Visual Leadership

Visual Leadership

The Church Leader As ImageSmith

ROB WEBER

ABINGDON PRESS
Nashville

VISUAL LEADERSHIP
THE CHURCH LEADER AS IMAGESMITH

This book is printed on acid-free, recycled paper.

**Cataloging-in-publication information applied for with the
Library of Congress**

ISBN 0-687-07844-X

Scripture verses marked NIV are from the New International Version of the Bible, © by The International Bible Society. Used by permission.

Unless otherwise noted, Scripture verses are from the New Revised Standard Version of the Bible, © Copyright 1989 by permission of the National Council of Churches in Christ USA. All rights reserved.

Line Illustrations by Cari Bennett Bollinger. Cari earned her B.A. in Fine Arts from Louisiana State University in Shreveport. She lives and creates in her studio in Shreveport, Louisiana, with the love and support of her husband Pete and son Nicolas.

For my wife Anita, my companion in life
For my son Jonathan, my partner in storytelling

Acknowledgements

The list of people who have shaped my understanding and have contributed to the formation of this book are more than can be numbered here, so I thank all those I name and the many who I cannot name. First, thanks to Anita, my wife, my patient one, the love of my life, and my grammar queen. I thank my son Jonathan, my partner in storytelling and adventure. He reminds me of the joy of creativity and the hope for tomorrow. I am especially grateful to Anita and Jonathan for their love and for letting me go write. I thank my father, Dr. Theodore R. Weber, for being patient with me as I struggled with the importance of creatively and faithfully appropriating the richness of our tradition in the context of a rapidly changing society. I thank my mother, Mudie Weber, for encouraging my creativity and my love for the natural world and for nurturing the spirit of the child. Thanks to my friend, Stacy Hood, for encouraging me in many ways and for helping me continue by transcribing and untangling some of the stories I told so that they could be committed to paper. Thanks to my editor at Abingdon, Paul Franklyn, who kept me writing after my automobile accident and encouraged me to get back on the horse. Thanks to Judy P. Christie for help and encouragement, and for the use of her "Camp Slower Pace" on the lake in the Cypress trees. Finally, I thank the wonderful staff and people of Grace Community United Methodist Church in Shreveport, Louisiana, for giving me a rich opportunity for leadership, and for allowing me to keep pace with the drummer I hear.

CONTENTS

Foreword

Ministry in the United States in the twentieth century was shaped by the trends and events of the nineteenth century. The westward expansion of the nation, new waves of immigration from Europe, the rise of the cities, the schisms in American Protestantism, the Civil War, emancipation of the slaves, the building of the railroads, the emergence of the public school system for the delivery of tax-funded educational services, the growth of manufacturing as a central component of the national economy, the numerical growth of the Methodists, Baptists, and Roman Catholics, the founding of hundreds of institutions of higher education, and that huge boom in the organization of new congregations following the Civil War were among the forces that created the context for ministry in the twentieth century.

What happened during the twentieth century that has transformed "how we do church in the twenty-first century"? That question requires a book length response, not a paragraph. Among the many changes the widespread ownership of the private automobile, cheap gasoline, good roads, two World Wars, the availability of low priced electricity, the rise of egalitarianism, the founding of thousands of nondenominational Christian congregations, urbanization, affluence, the emergence of the United States as this planet's only superpower, the new religious reawakening that began in the 1960s, consumerism, immigration to the United States from Mexico, Latin America, and the Pacific Rim, the extended life expectancy of forty-year-olds, and commercial air travel rank among the top twenty influential trends and events of the century just ended.

If the focus is narrowed to the one change that has transformed the role and duties of the parish pastor, the answer is clear. For nearly all of American church history, the primary channels for proclaiming the Gospel of Jesus Christ were the

9

spoken word and the printed word. By the end of the twentieth century, however, the most effective channel was visual imagery. One consequence is the change in the title for the clergy serving congregations. The old titles were minister, priest, pastor, and preacher. The successor, as Rob Weber points out in this book, is the ImageSmith.

From a larger perspective, a parallel change is the new definition of the pastor as leader. The twentieth century affirmed roles identified by such terms as "transformational leader" or "directional leader" and "visionary leader." All three are useful and appropriate in an ecclesiastical environment organized around the spoken word and the printed word.

If, however, that religious context requires planned change initiated from within the organization, a more useful term is found in the title of this book. The leader, who utilizes the benefits of visual communication, including shared stories, can be more effective with less stress than the change agent who ignores the power of visual imagery.

Like most contemporary discussions of leadership, this one reflects the personality of a particular leader. The distinctive contribution, however, is not in the life or personality of Rob Weber. That is an interesting story in itself. The reason to read this book, however, is to learn how to be an ImageSmith, how to be a visual leader, and how to be an effective pastor in a culture increasingly organized around visual imagery as the central channel of communication.

LYLE E. SCHALLER
Naperville, Illinois

Introduction

The context of leadership has changed. With the change comes new tools and new techniques, yet the heart of the leader remains constant. The leader's heart requires sensitivity to surroundings, an awareness of purpose and place, and an ability to use a variety of tools necessary to communicate with those who want to be led. Above all else, leadership is a *visual art*. What do I mean by that? Leadership is visual in that it requires an ability to envision the future into which you must lead. The leader must not only be able to see the vision, but be able to describe the vision in such a clear and compelling way that those influenced by his or her leadership will willingly offer their time, resources, and energy to live out the vision.

This book examines the process of leadership that is a "visual" art, which is proven effective in the congregational laboratory. My laboratory is Grace Community United Methodist Church (www.gracehappens.org), but it will become obvious that these visual principles can be applied in a variety of settings, because they are based on a communication strategy that fosters congregational ownership over the mission and strategies of the congregation.

While there is modest theoretical insight in this book, it is not intended as an introductory academic work, which typically surveys, digests, and translates the field of leadership studies into a congregational context. Ministerial students, however, would benefit from exposure to a visual form of leadership, because it fits the local church context well and it needs less translation than a sociological or psychological survey will offer. The book is aimed at practitioners who are providing leadership in Christian community, lay, clergy, or ministerial students.

Through this book, I intend for readers to gain:

❖ A better understanding of the nature of change within the congregation and the resulting struggle between groups within the congregation.

❖ Access to and understanding of several tools and the practices for effective leadership and communication in a postmodern media-saturated culture.

❖ A deep understanding of the dimensions and sources of human and congregational story that must be in balance if healthy change and growth is to occur.

❖ Examples of what can happen when the gifts and the abilities of those inside the congregation are released to tell the story in new and creative ways.

❖ A healthy connection to the sources of tradition and heritage without enslavement to particular modes of communication, organization, and expression, which may have been effective in the past.

❖ Encouragement for the task of leadership in this time of tremendous disruption and challenge for your congregation.

Several unintended consequences of previous solutions beset the congregation in our present situation. The maintenance mode for ministry is a problem because younger generations are looking elsewhere for spiritual nourishment, while the older members are dying. Congregations within a saturated region compete, define turf, and cancel out one another. Denominational bureaus struggle among and within themselves, defining boundaries or claiming turf. Church growth, by any means, causes a crisis of integrity in church leadership.

The diversity present in the different age groups and backgrounds that might come together on any particular Sunday to worship poses a different set of problems. Leadership in this time of diversity and fragmentation is a task that provides some unique, difficult, and extremely rewarding challenges.

Scattered, smothered, and covered

At the Waffle House, you can order your hash-brown potatoes either neatly fried in a disc, or "scattered, smothered, and covered": scattered on the grill, smothered in onions, and covered with cheese. In decades past, our experience in the church was much more typically homogenous and culturally controlled, but over the past quarter of a century, we were dislodged from the mirage of comfortable experience; we were left *scattered* from roots, family, and historical placement, *smothered* in a glut of information and images, and *covered* with frantic activity and opportunity. We are living in a time of an overwhelming media and information wave. We have more choices on digital cable or satellite for our viewing pleasure than we know what to do with and very little time to sit and watch. News streams at us real-time from the other side of the earth, we have books, e-mails and magazines (general and targeted), pagers, cell phones, handheld computers, and it is hard to assimilate all this information.

While the economy expands and contracts with the explosion of technology, media, and information access, we also are pummeled by a time of great cultural fragmentation. One unintended consequence for the current multisensory media explosion is that the phenomenon serves to create an entire world of "separate reality." Media and information streams create mental worlds in which it is possible to intellectualize experience and thus live disconnected from the realities of natural life, historical memory, and social interaction. When our realms of shared experience are movies, soap operas, or TV commercials, but we don't know our neighbors, we are by Christian definition losing touch with reality.

In the past the congregation faced geographic challenges as it sought to reach out to communities in different locations. It faced demographic challenges as neighborhoods and cities ebbed and flowed with ethnic migration and the rings of suburban racism. It faced generational challenges as new generations emerged to defy their parents and seek different approaches to work, style, community, and spirituality. None of these inherent forces will disappear, but on top of the already complex force-field comes the newest challenge: a transformation of the human mind through natural adaptation to multiple sources of information and diverse forms of media presentation. Mitchell Stephens, in *The Rise of the Image, the Fall of the Word*[1] writes of video, "It has the potential to take us to new mental vistas, to take us to new philosophic places, as writing once did, as printing once did." Digital imagery and multimedia communication are no passing fads. They are a new way of communicating and therefore must be claimed as a distinct visual method for sharing the Gospel.

As the church struggles to meet the disruptions from the last quarter of a century, so many alarm bells have rung that it is passé to claim that we live in crisis and cry out for renewal or rebirth. In this time of overlapping if not fractured worldviews, *this book is a guide for a new kind of leader, an ImageSmith.* Our situation calls for leaders who can speak to diverse perspectives or personalities and help point beyond the fragmentation to a larger narrative context.

From whence we've come

The church has faced times of major disruption, decline, and rebirth before. One approach to confronting change and rebuilding the effectiveness of the church in North America and sometimes Western Europe was the Revival. The revivalist approach to stirring up people and rebuilding the congregation was generally centered around a highly emotional event and a challenging preacher who would evoke a response of commitment from the crowd as it was moved on an emotional plane. The practice helped form congregations through the Great Awakenings and subsequently was effective as a communication or maintenance tactic in the short run. Congregations would see increases in attendance and membership, but the internal leadership system did not change to sustain the growth.

A more systemic approach emerged to certify the standardization of training for leadership. The goal of this academic model is to provide continuity of training and theology for distribution throughout the denominational system. The hope was that with a corps of consistently trained priests and reflective theologians (made in the image of the professor), the life of the church would be maintained and developed faithfully. The effectiveness and orientation of particular congregations would not be dependent upon particularly flamboyant revivalists or other charismatic leaders. The increased quality of education for parish ministers provided many benefits for the church and helped keep it from being blown around by every change in the surrounding culture. This model created congregations filled with well-informed listeners and, as specialization escalated, well-trained consumers of ordained professional ministry.

To supplement the academic approach to the development of congregations and the nurture of effective leadership, several experts assessed the congregation through the lenses of the social sciences and the business management schools. Congregational criticism developed an understanding of the sociology of religious institutions, and it provided valuable information about the subcultures within congregations and denominations. Some writers devised guidelines on how to develop evangelism programs and systems of care, with growth objectives. These leaders opened the doors to a renewed emphasis on high-quality programming. We were taught how to give appropriate attention to the systemic barriers to attracting and retaining new visitors and members. Social science analysis raised the awareness of the pattern of church decline corresponding to the lack of new church development. This analysis brought forth the need for the development of large numbers of new congregations to reach out to new populations who are not currently attending church.

Analysis of those who were staying away from church led to the development of churches targeted to attract new members with different styles of worship, music, and communication. As new types of churches developed by changing forms of communication and communications methodologies, conflict arose between the previous tier of "traditional" churches that saw the new churches as selling out to popular culture.

This book will not rehash the situation of the church sociologically, or provide possible directions for renewal or rebirth through management practices. These themes are well covered by church experts who understand the force field more clearly than I. *Visual Leadership* **is not** a "Jethro" (Moses' father-in-law, the one with the MBA) approach to organizing ministry tasks when providing leadership in a growing congregation. While management approaches to organizational culture deserve credit where results are measurable, they tend to focus on the troubleshooting, problem-solving, and maintenance of existing organizational systems. In this book, rather than Jethro, I depend more by analogy on the leadership strategies of two very different biblical characters, Ezekiel and Jesus. During times of accelerated disruption their practices opened people's eyes to the larger and new reality of God's story and invited them to enter the story. This approach to leadership development and practices facilitates the development of the visionary, Kingdom oriented perspectives. Storytelling and ImageSmithing are key practices in this leadership model.

The power of story

Many books are published on the role of narrative in the development and identity of congregations. Stanley Hauerwas' book, *The Peaceable Kingdom*,[2] establishes the setting for theology and ethics as participation in the unfolding narrative of God's work in the world. And there is in his view no salvation for the world apart from disciplined life in a congregation. Scripture provides the context for self-understanding and identity from which come our patterns of purpose and activity. James Hopewell in *Congregation: Stories and Structures*[3] dives deeper into the analysis of different types of narratives operating in congregational makeup and culture. He explores narrative as a matrix for understanding the structure and life of particular (increasingly unique) congregations. Story is more than simply descriptive narrative, however. Hopewell sees it as a forming and transforming force in the life of the congregation. "A healthy congregation, like a healthy family, is one that understands and tells its stories... A vital congregation is one whose self-under-standing is not reduced to data and programs but which instead is nurtured by its persistent attention to the stories by which it identifies itself" (Hopewell, 193). Story is the living being of the congregation that has formative and transformative abilities.

Richard Bondi examines the role of story in leadership from a different perspective, and its urgency cannot be overestimated. The hearing, telling, and placement of stories are the primary and most important activities of the leader. In *Leading God's People* he describes the task of the leader as knowing the story of the community, but not staying so deeply in the center of the community that he or she loses touch with the surrounding world.

> The leaders living most fully on the edge are those who can hear new voices and tell new stories. Such leaders hear the stories in their own community who have been thrust so far out on the edge as to be invisible from the center. They hear voices of other communities witnessing to the good that leads them on. Most profoundly, (and most dis-turbingly), they hear voices that make telling new stories inevitable and cast such a new light on real-ity that transformation is irrevocable even where its implications are incompletely worked out. None of the great and compelling stories that give order to our complex world are told in one voice. One of the things that keep great leaders on the edge is their capacity, sometimes experienced as a curse, to hear new voices and tell new stories.[4]

Narrative and story are not simply tools for congregational self-understanding, or the acts of reminiscence, introspection, or nostalgic longing. Story is a powerful source and strategy for leadership.

I could not do my work without the valuable analysis of congre-gational systems and the nature of programming that is required in various settings. We continually seek further understanding about internal systems and application of management tools, such as demographics, environmental analysis, and a clearer perception of our strengths, weaknesses, opportunities and threats.

Visual Leadership suggests that we need additional skills to overcome the challenges and disruptions before us. The best thinking about the congregation as a system, an organization, or a loose confederation of participants bound by a common cause will not quite get the leader past the barriers and pitfalls. Often church consultants mention in the recipe for a successful congregation that church boards or search committees should hunt for "an exceptional communicator" to lead their congregation. We could but we will not revive the perennial debate about "nature and nurture" when it comes to communication abilities or gifts for a leader. *Visual Leadership* will instead offer leaders strategies and examples of how to nurture their communication as ImageSmiths. The first lesson is to recognize that your story is a living and organic entity that takes place in a larger narrative setting within the congregation that you lead. Later we will be reminded that the role of the congregational leader is not simply to perpetuate the institution, keep it growing, and continue to tell the same stories over and over. Usually the leader will find ample opportunities to tell a new story that disturbs those he or she is called to lead.

Story is not simply recognized and celebrated as the rich, shared universe of understanding in which we live. Story is much more a powerful resource for congregational and community leadership. *The task of the ImageSmith is to create a community of StoryDwellers and StoryTellers.*

Diverse context, diverse community, diverse communication

This era is a time of complexity and fragmentation. It is a time that cries out for connection. This situation begs not for the specialists but rather for the *"globalists."* The church calls for "renaissance" leaders who are able to incorporate many dimensions of life, understanding, technology, and opportunity to create systems of thought and image that will allow people spiritual access and provide them with an *opportunity to see a greater reality than they currently understand.* Leaders must not only invoke an *intellectual understanding* of an opportunity and how to solve it, but also an *emotional investment* and connection so that the people will in turn be motivated internally to exercise free will, offer material resource, and infuse energy to create the future.

Leaders will be *able to function in the midst of varied perspectives,* not looking for absolute unanimity of belief and understanding, but instead attempting to build a framework of possibility that is linked to a variety of distinct "receptor sites," which people from many different backgrounds can grasp.

We will develop a *willingness to communicate in different ways, affirming the uniqueness of individuals,* so that we can enter the worlds of those to whom we are called. It is crucial that we not only learn the skills of proclamation that have dominated the church since its beginning, speaking and writing, but we must also develop skills and expertise in *communication through the power of the image by using the tools that are provided to us through technological innovation.* A leader in our current multisensory and multicultural society will lead through engaging people in the multisensory world of images. This kind of leadership requires skills in storytelling and media.

During the modern era, it seemed natural to segment and compartmentalize the different dimensions of human experience and life. Natural science was seen as a terrible contradiction to religious experience. The life of the spirit was viewed as disconnected from the life of the body. The modern experience was seen as something separate from and more advanced than the ignorance and superstition of those in our distant as well as immediate history. Scripture, to be trusted, must be dissected, interpreted, and explained in such a way that it "fit" into the modern interpretation of historical events.

Postmodernity is no cure for the failures of Modernity; it simply is a word for what filled the vacuum after a major collapse in Western civilization, when the imagined center failed to hold.

Diversity is now the best adjective to describe the church leader's situation. If the leader is to communicate effectively in the midst of tremendous diversity, found inside nearly any type of congregation, the focus should not be on a segmentation of truth, but rather on *weaving together the various strands of human experience so that the experience of reality becomes much more cohesive.* If the weaving succeeds, we call it community.

As technology and media forms explode and shatter many artificial barriers erected since the Reformation, we *understand the need for our connection to the ancient narrative sources of who we are as well.* The leader must develop sensitivity to a *variety of media forms* as well as an understanding of *multiple layers in story.* The use of media, image, and experience in communication is not simply a leadership tool that is applied like a software application to the raw information that will be conveyed, and targeted toward the goals of a particular organization or group. *Visual leadership* uses not only a diversity of communications forms but also teases out the multiple strands of human experience, which are shared with those who are part of the group that called us forth as leader.

Through reading *Visual Leadership*, you may be encouraged to look beyond the fractures and the confusion that color our diversity to reclaim and weave the larger story.

On the front cover and above in the introduction I refer in the subtitle to an ImageSmith. I am willing to explain what ImageSmith means for a church leader, as you move into Chapter One.

Notes

[1]Mitchell Stephens, *The Rise of the Image, the Fall of the Word* (New York: Oxford University Press, 1998), p. xii.

[2]Stanley Hauerwas, *Peaceable Kingdom: A Primer in Christian Ethics* (Notre Dame: Notre Dame University Press, 1983).

[3]James F. Hopewell and Barbara G. Wheeler, eds., *Congregation: Stories and Structures* (Minneapolis: Fortress Press, 1987).

[3]Richard Bondi, *Leading God's People: Ethics for the Practice of Ministry* (Nashville: Abingdon Press, 1989), p. 78-79.

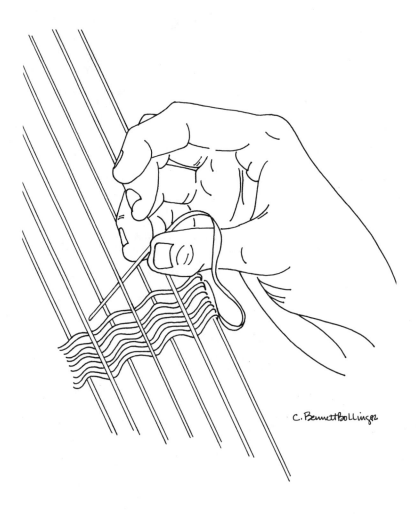

C. Bennett Bollinger

CHAPTER ONE

Weaver Woman, Crazy Priest, and the Voice of God

Her hands were calloused and stained by hard work, long life, and the colors of the yarn. The wooden shuttle passed rapidly with the appearance of ease through the white woolen strands attached to the frame of the loom. Almost as if emerging magically before me, through the quick and careful skill of the weaver—the spinning spools of yarn, rich, deep, colorful and vibrantly unique—came together, forming a beautiful design. The weaving was not only beautiful; it drew me in. "What is that design?" Its story told of light, darkness, beginnings and the place of the creature in the process of creation. There on the dusty side street in the shade of the old tin roof, wool, color, thread, skill and memory came together to create a form that silently issued a call. It was an invitation, at once, both to remember and to take one's place in that story that has been told, is being told, and longs to be told again. In her art and in the very activity of creating was a reflection of the substance of being, the process of becoming and the *heart at the center of wholeness*—an expression of dancing diversity, process and interplay, and the sharing of a sacred center.

An old Native American woman sitting on a stool on a dusty side street, separated from the days of her people's past by relocation to a reservation and a removal of the spirit of freedom, engages in an activity that tells the story of an enduring worldview which connects her to both a proud past and a future hope.

23

In another time and another place there was a similar activity that occurred on the street of a town in which people found themselves in exile. God's people had been turned out of the Promised Land and scattered in captivity in Babylon. It was there that a man who had trained for a priestly vocation in the Temple was found lying on the ground, drawing on a soft clay shingle a picture of the city, playing with homemade toy chariots, soldiers and, battering rams. As he attacked the clay drawing of the city with his little toy soldiers, he held an iron pan in front of his face so he could not see the city. He was doing just what he had been told to do by God.

> Now, son of man, take a clay tablet, put it in front of you and draw the city of Jerusalem on it. Then lay siege to it: Erect siege works against it, build a ramp up to it, set up camps against it and put battering rams around it. Then take an iron pan, place it as an iron wall between you and the city and turn your face toward it. It will be under siege, and you shall besiege it. This will be a sign to the house of Israel. (Ezekiel 4:1-3)

Those passing by stopped to see this strange occurrence. Some shook their heads and walked away, "He's gone crazy." Others stopped to wonder and to stare. Finally, someone had the courage to ask, "Ezekiel, what are you doing? Have you gone crazy? Get up and get out of the sun. I think it has gone to your head." The attention and the inquiry provided the opportunity for which Ezekiel had been waiting, and while they were still gathered and listening, he spoke words from the very *voice of God*, calling them home to a common *memory*, a common *life,* and a common *future.*

A weaver woman, a crazy priest, and the voice of God . . . what is going on here? What do they have in common? What they share is a common activity. Like a blacksmith who combines heat, force, and skill with metal in order to bring forth a horseshoe, a sword, or a plowshare, the weaver woman and the crazy priest were dancing with God, life, and story, and creating an image of a larger reality that provided grounding, purpose, and hope for them and their people. They are ImageSmiths.

What is an ImageSmith?

An ImageSmith is one who helps construct a framework of story through image that enables people to share a common vision of who they are and what it is that they are to accomplish. Ezekiel created a vivid image that grasped the attention of the people. He told a story in a strange way, but it had the desired effect. He told a story that changed the way that they understood where they were, who they were, and where they were going. Ezekiel was chosen by God to awaken in the people an understanding that they were far from where God wanted them to be. He was called to begin the process of leading them home, and to do so, Ezekiel acted as *ImageSmith*, forging a new sense of shared understanding and thus shaping their future.[1]

Not all ImageSmiths are leaders in the church, but the power of the ImageSmith to shape understanding, evoke creativity, and call forth deeper life in individuals and community is significant. *ImageSmithing* as a metaphor for church leadership can provide the basis for teaching (adults, children, and youth), community development, as well as for preaching and worship design. When the ImageSmith opens the story for others in the community, and when people catch a glimpse, they are changed. When they have seen the story, they begin to see everything with new eyes, and they in turn want to share the story with others.

Jesus was an ImageSmith, too. Jesus painted pictures with parables, fish, coins, birds, lilies, seeds, salt, and lamps. He built for us an image world that provided windows into the Kingdom. These images helped those who would follow Jesus to move toward abundant living. The activity of Jesus' leadership as creating an image of Kingdom was important because the Kingdom is not simply something one believes in, or understands, but is an environment where one lives. This Kingdom is incarnated through Jesus. As Jesus opens the story of Kingdom to those around him, and they began to see it, they wanted to share the environment as well.

ImageSmith and story

What, for this weaver woman, is the *substance of her reality*? Is it the dusty street on which she works? Is it the latest information coming across the news service ticker on CNN? Is it the modern scientific interpretation of physical and biological reality? Or is it story—the story told on the cloth that she weaves? While the first three things are part of the life that goes on around her, the substance of her reality is found elsewhere. *The substance of reality for her is found in that sacred story that forms her history, her here and now, and her hope.*

There are many threads of information and experience that make up who she is and define her life, but the thing that provides a foundation is that formational story told over and over by her ancestors as a reminder of her identity and her place in the world. She lives in the context of a story that provides meaning for her life and for her extended community. In other words, she and her tribe dwell in the same story. They are *storydwellers*.

The Israelites, too, were storydwellers. They were a people who shared the story of the creation, and the stories of Noah, Abraham, Egypt, the Exodus, the wandering and the settling of the Promised Land. They were people who shared the experience of the Temple of God being built in the center of their land and the fulfillment of the promises of God. They were dwellers in the story of God's activity in the world and of their place in the world in relation to God. Something happened to them when they were deported in waves to Babylon. They had to leave their sacred place and were spread out in a foreign land among a foreign people. They dwelt among those who lived in a different world, a different place, and a different story. As they were scattered, they began to forget the central place of their story.

When a small Hebrew child asked a question about who he was, or why the family performed a certain ceremony, or how the world worked, the elders would respond by telling the story. The stories served as a roadmap of where they had been, why they were where they were, and where it was that they were going. In one sense they told the stories as a way of remembering. Yet, in another sense, because they realized the importance of story as the framework of their universe, they didn't just *tell* the stories, they *dwelt* in the story. The story had life, and as they lived in its power, *the story began to tell them*—to shape their lives and their community. It was as if the life of the story was able to live them into being. In their *storytelling* and in their *storydwelling*, they found the ongoing link to God's purpose and activity in the world. The story sustained and directed them.

The problem of multiple stories

The amount of information we receive and the different opportunities for experience increase dramatically every day. It is amazing how much information is presented to us on a regular basis. While my parents were growing up, they received information from relatively few sources. There was a simple matrix of reality: parents and grandparents, school, books, church, limited radio, and perhaps a newspaper and a Sears catalogue. The story strands that made up the reality matrix were established, cohesive, and widely shared. Now, the reality matrices of our experience are much more complex. More diverse and multifaceted webs of story and information make up our experience. We have direct and immediate access to the breaking news that is happening all over the planet. Through the Internet, we can search for or research anything from how to make a basket to how to make a bomb. Access to almost all cultures, philosophies, religious systems, and special interest groups are just a few clicks away. The Internet is not simply a passive source of information (waiting for us to go to it); it is coming to us through the push of "spam" e-mail and info tracing and pop-up adds. We are awash in a storm of stories, images and information. People today live in a complex world of competing stories. In the book *Leading God's People*, Richard Bondi writes: "We live in a world where different stories of what it means to lead a good life compete for our hearts." (Bondi, p.10)

With the advent of TV and the rapid dissemination of cable programming and access to the Internet, we are more and more subjected to a story that beckons us into a world of perceived need and the desire for more. Pictures are painted of happy people who wear the right deodorant or drive the right car. In this story, we are motivated to respond to a projection of a reality that has been constructed by marketing gurus whose job it is to convince us that we need these products and will experience life more abundantly if we buy them. Part of the negative connotations that accompany our participation in the world of consumerism and advertising is that we are given a false sense of security through products. We are sent the message that money equals meaning, or that access to spending power—even if it is through increased debt—is a passport to a rich and satisfying existence. This message re-emphasizes the importance of the rat race: work more to earn more to buy more, which leads to the need to work more.

Leadership and ImageSmithing

The stories we receive as our own shape the way we see reality and the way that we live out our lives. The task of the ImageSmith is to create new images which bring God's story into focus as the central story. As the leader tells the story of God in the community and as the story is rehearsed and remembered, people become mindful of who they are, who they are to be, and perhaps, who they can become. As the story is understood, it informs the history, present, and future of the community, and shapes celebrations, rites of passage, and dreams.

As Richard Bondi writes, "Leaders hear powerful stories and tell them to those s/he is called to lead." (p. 64) The act of storytelling with the purpose of shaping the understanding and behavior of a group is a leadership activity. Stories provide the conceptual context for life. They express the images by which we interpret our trek through time. Stories, though, not only define reality, but also help to shape and create reality as well. Jesus told stories that drew people into new ways of thinking, being, deciding, living, and forming community. This type of storytelling is an activity of leader. Jesus painted pictures with parables that provided windows into the Kingdom. These images helped those who would follow Jesus move in the direction of Kingdom living. The activity of Jesus' leadership as creating an image of Kingdom was important because the Kingdom was not simply something to be believed in, or understood, but lived in, and thus incarnated.

Something I learned from my grandfather

My grandparents, especially my grandfather on my mother's side, shaped my understanding of the colors and rhythms of the natural world. I remember riding from Georgia to Connecticut in an old VW square-back, arriving late at night because we didn't want to spend an extra night on the road, and there, through the porch into the door and that smell... the old wooden house smell. The house was a farmhouse that was built in the 1800s. My grandfather was one of my heroes. He was an immigrant from Sweden. He was a farmer, philosopher, and an artist. He never did say much, but he taught me an awful lot. There was something magnetic about him.

I loved to go to the farm in the summer. I would follow him around as he did his work, and in that interaction, I learned much. I watched him prepare soil for planting. I watched and helped him plant. I helped pick vegetables. I saw him work with his grape arbor, and he showed me how he made wine. He showed me how to grow tomatoes and corn and cucumbers. He taught me the right kinds of things to mix in the soil so that it wasn't too clumpy and it wasn't too sandy.

I was drawn to him and I could sit with him for hours. He never said much, but he taught me so much. One of the neatest experiences I remember having with him was going down into the basement of the house. This was a really cool basement. One day, we had been outside in the garden digging, gathering vegetables, and talking about the seasons. We came inside for something and I followed him down the creaky wooden plank steps into a plaster- and dirt-walled cellar. The cellar was filled with all kinds of things: a wine press, huge five-gallon bottles in which he made the wine, and shelves filled with jars of preserved vegetables from the garden, ready for winter.

In the center of the basement floor was an old potbellied wood-burning stove. The stove was used to heat the house and to provide hot water. This was intriguing to me, as I had never thought of having to do something to heat the house or the water except to change the thermostat or turn the faucet. I stayed close to him and watched.

It seemed like a place that was beyond my normal experience of time. I watched as he gathered up some wood scraps, opened the door of the furnace, and fed the wood in. The flames were bright in the stove and I was amazed at the way he could put his hands quickly into the flames to arrange the wood without being burned. The light of the flames illuminated his deeply tanned and furrowed skin.

After he had finished feeding the stove, he turned, looked at me, and said, "Let me show you something." He pulled the chain on the light bulb that hung down on a wire from the beam above us. The cellar darkened. He opened the stove door again and the light of the fire glowed warmly into the room. He walked to the center of the room where a large lead ball, about the size of a grapefruit, hung on strong twine from the rough wooden beam above. The ball hung just a foot or so above the floor. He knelt and gave the ball a spin. It was spinning on the end of the twine. The light of the stove was glowing on one side of the ball and he said, "This is the way the earth is spinning in space, and the light of the sun shines on the earth making day and night."

Then he stood and grasped the twine towards the top and moved it in a little circular motion parallel with the floor. This caused the ball not only to spin, but also to begin to travel in a smooth, swinging, orbital motion. "See how it tilts and gets closer to the flames. That is summer, and when it tilts away, that is winter. When it is here, it is the spring. Is when I plant. You come to see me when it is here. This is the way the seasons work." In a cool, damp old basement, with a potbellied stove, some twine and a lead ball, he enlarged my perspective on the universe.

In one short moment—the image of how the planets and the seasons worked—a whole new perspective on the universe was opened to me and connected with the joy of helping bring forth life from the ground. When I got back to Georgia, I wanted to share the joy of seeds, plants, and the miracle unfolding of life with others. I planted popcorn in soup cans and went up and down the street giving it to all the neighbors. Before that experience, popcorn kennels were just little things waiting to be placed in a pan with oil, popped, and eaten. After the story of creation and the rhythms of nature were opened to me, I saw those same kernels as capsules of life and growth. *Somehow I believe this is part of the reason I want to share the joys of life and growth today.* He probably didn't know it, and neither did I at the time, but as I watched, I saw a picture of a loving, creative, good man who had his hands in it all, helping it to be ordered. *In some way, I believe he helped me with my perspective on God.* And I want to share it with others. That is the power of the ImageSmith.

What I must do as a church leader

One of the most important tasks of a church leader today is to help God's people find *shared memory*, *community*, *purpose* and *direction*. If a congregation shares these four things, then leading will be helping to steer something that is already moving in the right direction. If the congregation does not share these things, leading will be more like herding cats and dragging a dead elephant while carrying on a conversation on a cell phone with call waiting (not a pretty picture, is it?).

Currently in the congregation I serve, a large number of people come from different religious traditions, or from little or no church background at all. It is important for us to help people understand what it is that we are all about as a church, so that they might decide to be a part of it. It is important that we have a shared understanding of who we are and where we are headed so that we can move without spending too much time and energy on internal conflict and bickering.

In order to set the stage and introduce life in the congregation, we have a gathering for people who want to learn what the church is about, and what membership means. We call the gathering "Discovering Grace." It is part of a process of learning and experiences designed to help people grow in faith and discipleship. The process is called *Pathways.*[2]

In the Pathways process, we try to hold up a clear understanding of the the scriptural story as the context for shared understanding. We try to provide people with a sense of historical connection to the development of the people of God through time. We also have developed a series of classes, retreats, and experiences that help the people gain tools for spiritual development and possibilities for response through service and deeper involvement in the continually unfolding story of God. In the rest of this book we will look at the process of helping people understand and live in the story of God in this complex time of multiple stories. One of the core stories we share is the *story of the shell.* The story provides us with a shared image and a tangible reference to who we are and what we are trying to do as a congregation.

The shell

Being asked to go start something new is a somewhat frightening task. It is at once frightening and exciting. When the district superintendent called and asked me if I would consider being the pastor of the new church start, I wanted to make sure that it was what God wanted me to do and not just something that looked new and exciting. My wife and I were trying to discern whether we should take the opportunity to move and be part of the planting of a new congregation, so we went down to the land and walked around. We walked across the area that used to be covered with trailers, many of the remnants still there. Then we climbed over the old barbed wire fence and walked into the towering pines. We talked about possibilities. We talked about the difficulty of leaving our current congregation. After a while we stopped to pray. I'm not one who usually asks for signs, but as we stopped to pray, I asked God to help me see what I was to do. I wanted to do what was the best thing for continuing to extend the Kingdom. We bowed to pray.

As we finished praying, I looked down at my feet, and there on the ground was a big pink conch shell half-buried in the pine straw. "Now, what is a big pink conch shell doing half-buried in the pine straw in the middle of some undeveloped, unimproved woods in North Louisiana?" I thought. I wasn't sure, but I picked it up and started to imagine.

If you have played at a coastal beach, you have almost certainly seen a hermit crab in one of the tourist shacks. They are those little fuzzy crustaceans that inhabit the discarded shells of other creatures. They find a shell, move in, eat, and grow. After they've scuttled around and eaten enough seaweed, they get big enough to need another shell, and if they don't find another shell, they cease to grow and eventually die. The decision to move is a critical point in the life of a hermit crab. If they decide to go to another shell, they risk moving beyond the protection of their present shell.

So, here I am standing in the woods looking at a shell, thinking, "O.K., I think the time has come for the body of Christ to have another shell." It wasn't about my ministry and me. It wasn't about me needing a larger church or a bigger challenge. It was about another shell for the Body of Christ. It was about an opportunity for that Body to grow and to stretch and to become a different form and a different shape.

Some may ask me how I knew that the shell was a message from God for me at that time. The truth is that I don't know what the shell was doing there, or whether or not it was some kind of sign from the divine. It very well could have been that Bubba and Lou Ann in one of the trailers next door had gone to Destin and they bought this thing as a reminder of their lovely trip to the beach. Maybe they kept it in a little rock garden outside the trailer door with other shells and rocks from places they had visited. And Bubba got mad at Lou Ann one night and stepped out on the back steps and picked up that special shell and thought, "I'll show her," and chunked her shell back out in the woods. Maybe

that's how it got there. Or maybe God planted it there in a particular way. Maybe God worked through Bubba and Lou Ann to
plant it there for just such a time as this. Who knows?

I don't know, but at that point, that shell spoke to me of the
opportunity to take a risk and to allow a new shell to be created so
that the body of Christ could develop and serve this community
and reach out to the world in new ways. To me that was a powerful image. I've stuck with it and figured if it wasn't God, then at
least it was a good story. I keep that shell in my office and bring it
with me every time I tell the story at Discovering Grace. I tell the
story over and over—and people remember—they remember that
we are about taking risks and trying to be the Body of Christ in
new ways in a new time and a new environment.

Where we are going

To get us oriented, here is a brief overview of the structure of
the book. First, we will look the prophet Ezekiel's situation as a
leader of people in exile, and examine his setting and task to
learn from the similarities with our time and task. From Ezekiel,
we will also learn from his model of leadership about using multiple images and activities to build shared memory and identity.

Chapters 4–7 develop the task of church leader as
ImageSmith, and examine Scripture, tradition, reason, and experience as the sources and structures of meaning we draw from to
create a matrix of shared story. By using the process of painting
a landscape as a guiding metaphor, we will explore how to layer
these sources and structures of meaning, keeping them in balance and perspective.

Chapters 8–10 develop some of the practical applications of
how to exercise leadership as ImageSmith in this digital age,
through vision, new media and ancient story.

Chapter 11 describes the activity of the ImageSmith as one
who gives away the story as well as the task of transmission so
that it can grow, thus creating a community of storydwellers and
storytellers. I will provide examples of the attempt to find this
balance, and suggestions for ways to keep close to the source of

the Story and to keep the light on.

Visual Leadership: The Church Leader as ImageSmith **is based on the understanding that we live in a world that is made up of story, and that understanding story, living story, telling story, and releasing story are key to providing effective leadership.** I pray that we all might catch a glimpse of the power, not simply in *telling stories,* but in *opening the Story* for those with whom you share in ministry.

Notes

[1] In biblical studies of the Hebrew prophets, these stories are often called *symbolic actions,* which function much like parables in New Testament times. Ezekiel and Isaiah, for example, draw on familiar objects to act out the parable, in a one-man skit, as an interpretation of the current predicament.

[2] *Pathways* is the name of our new member and discipleship formation process. For more information on Pathways, go to www.gracehappens.org.

C. Bennett Bollinger

CHAPTER TWO

Surveying the Landscape

Waking up to the reality of change

One of my favorite movies is *The Wizard of Oz*. I was frightened by some of the characters (mainly the flying monkeys) when I was a small child, but I was always intrigued by the way in which, after the tornado, Dorothy woke up in an entirely different place. The house stopped and the music became soft. Slowly she made her way to the door and looked out. When she opened the door and looked outside, she saw a world that was totally different from the one out of which she had come. The people were different, her situation was different, her enemies were different, her purpose became different (getting home) and even the way the world looked (now filmed in Technicolor) was different. When she came to her senses after that tornado and looked around outside, she said those famous words, "Toto, I don't think we're in Kansas anymore."

Where she had been had its own set of problems, but after the twister, she found herself faced with new surroundings and new types of people with very different perceptions of what the world was all about. She was faced with a different task. She needed to get home.

I can imagine that Ezekiel felt much the same way after being deported to Babylon. While his transportation to Babylon was not conveyed by tornado, and therefore was not quite as abrupt, the change was still every bit as traumatic. Upon arriving,

Ezekiel faced a changed situation, a changed audience, a changed purpose, and thus a changed way of going about his task. Let's examine some of the elements of the changes that Ezekiel faced and see how they might apply to our current situation in the life of the church.

A brackish situation

Ezekiel was trained in a very traditional setting. He was trained to be a priest in the line of all the priests who had gone before. He was prepared to carry on the practices of Temple sacrifice and ritual, to provide the community with a sense of interaction with the divine. The Temple and the activities of the Temple were central to the culture. The community was unified around the story that was told in every activity, every song, and every architectural feature of the Temple. He'd been born into a community that was centered on the Temple and a story that was centered in God. Things seemed so stable and so unlikely to change. His life was to be a life of caring for the rites and rituals of the Temple community, telling and retelling the story like so many had before him.

Ezekiel was most likely well prepared for the task that was before him. He had probably taken all of the right courses at the yeshiva (seminary) in preparation for his task: Ephod Maintenance, The Care and Sacrifice of Turtledoves, Discerning the Blemishes (otherwise known as "God don't want your bull!"), and Psalmody. He had all of the courses needed to fulfill the task of maintaining the functions of the Temple and telling the story that stood at the center of the community. Ezekiel, however, was not prepared for the changes that were about to take place all around him.

Even though things seemed stable in Israel, rumblings in the larger culture would affect them more than they could ever imagine. The Assyrian and Egyptian armies decided to have a war and use Israel as the battleground. The Israelites were deported in stages to Babylon. They were not enslaved. They were not mistreated. They were simply uprooted from their place and shifted to a different place—a place without the order provided by the centrality of the Temple. There in Babylon things were quite different. The Temple was no longer the anchoring point in the common experience of the people. The Israelites had been scattered and spread out and yet there were some positive aspects to their captivity. They were still allowed to participate in their religious rituals. They were still allowed to work and earn money. Even their king, the King of Israel, was allowed to live in a wing of the palace with the Babylonian ruler. He even may have had a favored tax status. All of these comforts contributed to the experience of the Israelites gradually beginning to feel as if there really wasn't that much wrong with being in captivity.

Many parallels exist between the situation of the Israelites and our own current situation. We may not have been exiled into another land, but we have awakened in a time and in a culture that constantly disrupts our expectations.

I once spent time on the South Georgia coast. My friend had a cabin on a tidal river. It was a great place. The little dock stuck out into the river, and at certain times of the day I could stand out there and throw a cast net and come up with shrimp. At other times there were no shrimp, but the water was filled with all kinds of other creatures. A tidal river is an interesting place. It is a place where two different environments, two different modes of life, meet. It is the joining of salt and fresh waters. When the tide is out, the river is flowing fresh water out into the ocean, but when the tide comes in, the river flows in the other direction and is salt water flowing in from the ocean. In the movement the two intermingle, and that area of intermingling is called "brackish."

Imagine the story of God that Israel lived by and the experience of that story in the Promised Land as a pond of pure freshwater, and imagine the Babylonian culture as a saltwater ocean. The people of Israel who were picked up from the pond of their own place and reality matrix centered in the story of God and were placed into the salt sea of the Babylonian culture. We too have experienced a transition, but the process has been different. The tidal river of culture and story has changed and shifted. We are in the same place, but the nature of the culture surrounding us is radically different. We look out the door of our church and home and expect to see one type of fish (you know, those Christian fish), and instead, we see shrimp and squid. It is not just that they are shrimp and squid, appearing differently and doing things differently, but they also live in a different type of water. The story in which they swim is from a different source. Our reality matrix becomes "brackish."

The shift, like that in Babylon, is not that the story of God has been disproved, or attacked, or outlawed. It simply lost central place in the culture, and thus became one story among many. The story waters intermingled. This shift from the story of God being the central story in the lives of people and the community as a whole to being one of the many stories that informed their reality matrix was gradually and almost imperceptibly devastating. This was a big problem for Ezekiel and for Israel. While they felt that they were still free to practice their religion, they were no longer centered in story.

We, like those in captivity, have experienced transition. I am not suggesting that *once upon a time* there was an idyllic period in which Christianity was followed apart from the pollution of our society, as if we lived in a purified pond of Christian water. We have always experienced diversity of belief and religious practices, and even (heaven forbid) dissension amongst different Christian groups. However, in many situations today, our churches are designed and organized to take care of maintaining a story in a particular story environment—a "pond" or a "lake" or even a "river"—each contain different critters, but the water is "fresh." Now we are discovering that the tides have changed and brought a whole new environment. We no longer live in the same type of world. Our situation has changed.

The difficulty for church leaders is that, like Ezekiel, we were prepared for one situation, but through no fault of our own, we have been thrust into a different setting. And to add to the difficulty, there is enough comfort to keep us from depending on God, enough opportunity to keep us from relying on God, enough distraction to keep us from being centered on God, and enough religion to quench any major spiritual longings.

Aquarium dwellers

Ezekiel was also confronted with a different type of audience for his message than he would have had back in the "good ole' days." In the days and years before the people were deported from the Promised Land, there was much more of a *common experience of life*. They lived together in the freshwater pond of the story of God. There was a pattern to the community experience based on the celebration of feast days and the more regular gathering for public worship. The rhythm of the community was set by the story at the center—the Temple and the presence of God. I understand that no matter how stable a community seems, changes are always taking place, yet at this time a greater feeling of continuity of experience prevailed from generation to generation.

As the setting changed, so too did the experience of the people. There were major differences in perspective based on how and when they experienced exile. Those who had lived the majority of their lives in the stability of the centrality of the Temple, had memories so strong that they continued to live in the understanding of God as stable, present, changeless, and always loving even when things were difficult. These people could hold on to the memory of the way it had been without having to acknowledge the total change that was surrounding them. They came to the Babylonian saltwater in a freshwater aquarium (and sometimes kept their curtains closed).

Another group of people were young when the exile began. As they grew and developed, their lives seemed to have more grounding in exile than in the memory of the Temple community. These people saw the world, the place of the people of God in the world, and the nature of the community in a very different way. Priests, rituals, and structures took on a much less important role. Perhaps even the very place of the story in the life of the individual began to diminish. There was still a hunger for God and a questioning about their present circumstances, but they were much more focused on the present than they were on the past. These people began to swim in the saltwater, but wore a vial of freshwater on a string around their neck and visited the aquarium on occasions.

Yet another group emerged. A growing group of people during the time of the exile had no memory at all of the days in the Promised Land, or were more attracted to the Babylonian customs and cultures than they were to the customs and cultures of what began to seem like "has been" religion. These folks lived in the saltwater and might glance into the aquarium out of curiosity.

In this context were three types of people: *aquarium dwellers,* people with Temple memory who were committed to the old ways; *aquarium visitors,* people with Temple memory who were beginning to feel pretty comfortable in the exile; and *saltwater dwellers,* those who had no memory of the centrality of the Temple or were quickly losing what little memory they did have.

When I look out at those who gather in worship at our church on any given weekend, I can see those same groups. I know where they sit, and you probably do too in your setting.

The *aquarium dwellers* remember the way it was. They are good people who love God deeply. Many of them are the builders and sustainers of the church.

The *aquarium visitors* believe in God and know that it is important to attend church, based on memories from Sunday school when they were kids. Now that they have children of their own, they want to make sure that their children get to visit the aquarium too for some spiritual rewards.

Most *saltwater dwellers* never come to church. If they do come, they might be there because they are made to come by their spouse, parent, or grandparent. Or they come in for a wedding or special event. They are spiritual beings and have a curiosity about spiritual things, but most of the time they don't look towards the church to answer their soul questions. Instead, they look to other places for spirituality: new age, mysticism, Eastern religion, nature religion, and so forth. Christianity and the church are foreign to them because they are from the *saltwater.*

They have no understanding of the Christian story or theology of the faith, but they know that it has something to do with getting married or buried. Most of the time they are more visible far away from the aquarium.

These existential differences translate into some practical effects that need to be understood if we are to effectively provide leadership for all these different creatures that inhabit this time of brackish spirituality.

Differences in musical styles

The difference in memory and experience also led to the diversity in musical style and lyrical content. There were those who remembered when they used to gather in the Temple and sing again those *great old songs* like "God's Love Endures Forever" (accompanied by the sons of Asaph and Korah on the trumpet, harp, and cymbals). There were also newer musicians who began to write out of their experience, not of the centrality of the Temple and the good ole days of the enduring love of the all-powerful God. Instead they wrote out of their experience of separation—their *angst*—their pain. I can imagine that the focus as well as the graphic nature of the lyrics of one of the songs that came out during the exile (hitting the top of the chart with the younger generation who longed for a deeper experience of God) seemed edgy and disturbing to the "God's Love Endures Forever" crowd. Imagine the parents of the young Israelites talking about their children as they hear them playing their new music, and worrying about them as they heard the words:

> "How can we sing the songs of God while we are in a foreign land? Remember, O LORD, what the Edomites did on the day Jerusalem fell. "Tear it down," they cried, "tear it down to its foundations!"
>
> O Daughter of Babylon, doomed to destruction, happy is he who repays you for what you have done to us—he who seizes your infants and dashes them against the rocks. (Psalm 137:7-9)

Think about the situation in so many of our churches. A clash evolves between different musical styles and tastes. These clashes aren't so much a question of who is right and who is wrong, who is faithful and who is not. It is a clash between two different ways of seeing the world in which we live and the place of the people of God in that world. [For more on this clash, see Stacy Hood, *Rekindling Your Music Ministry*, (Nashville: Abingdon, 2002) available as an eBook from cokesbury.com.]

The tide

Ezekiel was preparing to maintain and sustain the ongoing life of the Temple community but circumstances beyond his control brought him to a new place. In this new place, there was no Temple. In this new place the people were scattered. In this new place, his job description radically changed. In this new place, Ezekiel had to learn to communicate in a way that could attract and hold the attention of all of the diversity of perspective and perception that made up the people of God in exile. He had to communicate with a diverse and scattered people and he had to begin to form in them a sense of who they were together and what it was to which God was calling them.

His job was to begin to build in the minds of the exiled ones in their various forms, the beginnings of the renewed community that God was showing him as a path to the future: speaking to diverse perspectives in the middle of an exile. He was not simply trying to convince individuals to believe that there is a God, but also trying to get people to unite as community to live out the presence of God and the continued story of God's interaction in the world. This was Ezekiel's task. It was not an easy one, and I believe that this is much the same task that faces present-day leaders of congregations.

We are in a different place. The tide has changed and the culture in which we find ourselves has changed. In this new place, simply continuing to do what we have done in the past won't cut it. This new place requires a different understanding of the task facing the church. This new place requires a different understanding of the way we approach communication and worship design. This new place requires a different understanding and approach in the way we go about designing outreach and evangelism.

The tide has changed and we find ourselves in brackish water. In the next chapter, we will look at the power of story in the task of bringing healing, hope, and wholeness to our church in this brackish time.

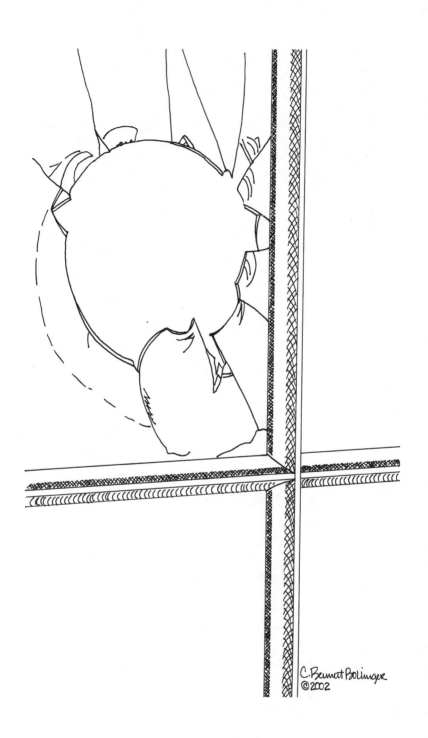

C. Bennett Bolinger
©2002

CHAPTER THREE

Scattered Shards, and the Healing Power of Memory and Story

The water rolled down his head and neck, and tears welled up in both of our eyes. When I looked up, I saw the tears that were present in the eyes of many in the congregation as well. He had come to the church seeking some kind of direction for a shattered life. Drug addiction, jail, and broken relationships were the elements of his experience. As he came, I introduced him to another member with some similar history—the story of addiction is a powerful one—and he was received with love and caring. Sharing stories of brokenness and pain with others who are making their journey through recovery has helped him begin to heal, to find purpose and direction, and to realize a need for community and accountability. As we gathered in the baptismal area that day, the light filtered through the stained glass casting rich colors on the bubbling fountain, the bowl, the pitcher, and the one who had come to take his place in the story of God. God's work was being done. Redemption and wholeness was happening. It was my job to tell the story in a way that we could understand. Our job as *ImageSmith* is lifting the memory and story so we can not only know the story but also see precisely how we fit in the story.

As we were building our first worship facility, we wanted to design a piece of stained glass that would express our life in

47

Grace and our connection to the Christian story. We envisioned a freestanding piece of glass art that would stand in the baptismal area. An artist in the congregation volunteered to share her gift by translating concept into image. We talked and prayed. When she brought me the design, I was overwhelmed. We took the design to a stained-glass artist who looked at the design, and then invited us to help select the glass that would be used in the creation. The artist has broken colored glass scattered around the studio, some in sheets, some shattered into several pieces. We looked and we chose the different pieces, textures, and colors. Broken and separate, the pieces of glass did not look like much. But as the different colors and textures were assembled into the artwork and their patterned diversity refracted the source of light, the image told a story that was complex and beautiful. The shards of glass, although of different type, age, consistency and color, as they are assembled in the context of shared story come together to become something more than they could be individually. Now the window stands as an expression of the faith of the designer and the congregation, and as an image inviting us into the truth of God's story.

Deep purple and blue points appear to be thrusting into the image from the top and the sides. The points represent the presence and activity of God as it enters the world mysteriously yet powerfully. The points are almost joined at the center, forming a cross. From the center of the cross flow green, blue, and white water; and woven into that flowing water is a single strand of vibrant red, the Blood of Christ. In that image is present the truth of our story that has been, is now, and ever will be. God loves enough to enter our world. God loves in such a way as to forgive us and accept us in all of our imperfection, and God's love offers to us not only cleansing and renewal, but also a source of abundant life and joy.

It was in front of that stained glass that we had gathered to baptize this man. As we stood there, we looked at that image and remembered, and we were also reminded that even in our diversity and once-brokenness, we come together to form an image through which the light of God shines into a darkened world. The brokenness and diversity tell our story, and as we remember, we see ourselves in the context of that larger story. As leaders, we help in assembling the pieces, telling the story, holding up the image of the larger whole so that we can find our place in the story.[1]

Shared memory and the act of sharing story have tremendous power to unify and to heal individuals and communities. Stanley Hauerwas describes the power of the story in the activity of redemption:

> "To be redeemed is to learn to place ourselves in God's history, to be part of God's people. To locate ourselves within that history and people does not mean we must have some special experience of personal salvation. Redemption, rather, is a change in which we accept the invitation to become part of God's kingdom, a kingdom through which we acquire a character befitting one who has heard God's call. Now an intense personal experience may be important for many, but such experiences cannot in themselves be substitutes for learning to find the significance of our lives only in God's ongoing journey with creation. (Hauerwas, *The Peaceable Kingdom*, p.33)

I believe that there is a personal dimension to redemption— but that it is dependent on context. In so much of the expression of Christianity, the nature of salvation is a moment of individual agreement with the truth claim of the Gospel. "Jesus died for you, a sinner, and if you confess and believe that he will save you, then you will get to go to heaven." This approach, I believe, adds to the number of people who are getting tickets for the bus ride to the afterlife rather than creating storydwellers and kingdom builders in this world that means so much to God. In this context, let's look again at Ezekiel.

Dem bones, dem bones, dem dry bones...

Ezekiel finds himself in a foreign land with a fragmented, scattered, broken, and diverse people. His world has changed. He is not prepared for what he is called upon to do. He needs to draw the people back together and encourage them to be faithful. He needs to find a way to awaken them from their relative comfort and distractions. When Ezekiel looked at the people he was to lead and saw the tremendous diversity of thought, experience, and connection to the past, I imagine he was somewhat daunted by the task of trying to communicate with them. Yet God, in a very creative and vivid way, shared an image with him of what was and what was to come.

> The hand of the LORD was upon me, and he brought me out by the Spirit of the LORD and set me in the middle of a valley; it was full of bones. He led me back and forth among them, and I saw a great many bones on the floor of the valley, bones that were very dry. He asked me, "Son of man, can these bones live?"
>
> I said, "O Sovereign LORD, you alone know."
>
> Then he said to me, "Prophesy to these bones and say to them, 'Dry bones, hear the word of the LORD! This is what the Sovereign LORD says to these bones: I will make breath enter you, and you will come to life. I will attach tendons to you and make flesh come upon you and cover you with skin; I will put breath in you, and you will come to life. Then you will know that I am the LORD.' "
>
> So I prophesied as I was commanded. And as I was prophesying, there was a noise, a rattling sound, and the bones came together, bone to bone. I looked, and tendons and flesh appeared

on them and skin covered them, but there was no breath in them.

Then he said to me, "Prophesy to the breath; prophesy, son of man, and say to it, 'This is what the Sovereign LORD says: Come from the four winds, O breath, and breathe into these slain, that they may live.' " So I prophesied as he commanded me, and breath entered them; they came to life and stood up on their feet—a vast army.

Then he said to me: "Son of man, these bones are the whole house of Israel. They say, 'Our bones are dried up and our hope is gone; we are cut off.' Therefore prophesy and say to them: 'This is what the Sovereign LORD says: O my people, I am going to open your graves and bring you up from them; I will bring you back to the land of Israel. Then you, my people, will know that I am the LORD, when I open your graves and bring you up from them. I will put my Spirit in you and you will live, and I will settle you in your own land. Then you will know that I the LORD have spoken, and I have done it, declares the LORD.' " (Ezekiel 37:1-14)

He saw the image of brokenness and fragmentation. He saw the image of death and apparent hopelessness, yet God called to him and asked him if he thought the bones could rise again. Playing it safe, Ezekiel answered respectfully, "Only you know such things...," but God wasn't letting his chosen leader off the hook so easily. Ezekiel wasn't going to get away with handing off responsibility for leadership to God. God commanded him to prophesy to the bones. But how will the bones rise if the leader fails to speak?

The concept of prophecy in the Hebrew Bible is widely misunderstood. The writings of the prophets in the Bible are often confused with apocalyptic literature, which is understandable, because sometimes prophets do perceive of history in apocalyptic terms. When apocalyptic writers are looking forward in history, they try to describe a future that represents the collapse of the past and a radical new beginning for God's people. Biblical prophecy, however, is not a mystical, symbolic telling of what is going to happen in the future. Prophecy in the Old Testament is defined as speaking the truth about two things: a) the current situation and b) God's story, drawing obvious conclusions and asking the hearers to make a choice.

Some readers can make a case that Ezekiel is describing a future reality for the nation, which would discard the past and rise again to start over completely. However, I think that Ezekiel was connecting the people, represented by the scattered bones with a memory of God's faithful, forgiving and redemptive story, and it was the power of that memory that gathered the dry bones and united them, filling them with purpose, direction, and hope. The resurrection of the dry bones is a powerful image for the activity of God in restoration and hope. The disjointed pieces scattered and lifeless are ordered and patterned and given life. For present-day Christians who gather in congregations, the bones are the memory of who we are in God's story, which heals us, unifies us, and gives our purpose and direction.

Memory and story as the substance of community

I heard a radio commentator, shortly after the 9/11 terrorist attacks in New York, Washington, and Pennsylvania, reflecting on the way in which so many people were rushing out to get a copy of the September 12, 2001 newspaper with the pictures of the Trade Center and the Pentagon and the "America Attacked" headlines. He reflected that while he thought the September 12th edition of the paper would become a collector's item, he believed that the real collector's item was the paper from the day before. He said it was the last paper of the old world. The stories in the September 11th edition of the newspaper painted a picture of a scattered people. The stories reflected tremendous division based on individualism and economics. On the day following the attacks, a different focus emerged. It was reported that this was the first paper of the new world. It showed a very different picture of America. A new unity and commitment prevailed. Perhaps it was partially due to the shocking shared experience, but I think that it was more than that. A unifying story drew people's experiences of reality back into line with one another and through that alignment, things began to be remembered: the flag, prayer, hugging your children, giving to help others. These fundamental realities of identity were brought back to the surface by the shared experience of terror and the shared memory of who we are as Americans. One person reflected that in New York City, where people rarely look each other in the eye, or speak unless there is a reason to speak, an openness and a sense of community arose, which previously had been invisible. The brokenness was overcome by the recovery of a shared memory—the memory of the values of community, sacrifice, service, caring, and love.

Current day prophecy and real resurrection

A powerful example of the healing and unifying power of shared story and the sharing of stories can be found at the corner of Taylor and Ellis streets in San Francisco, California. Glide Memorial UMC was a church in the center of a huge and growing city, and yet like so many churches in transitional neighborhoods, it was in decline and not reaching the people in the surrounding community. The community surrounding the church is known as the "Tenderloin." The Tenderloin is the center of all things illegal in San Francisco. It is an area known for drugs, prostitution, and homelessness. Reverend Cecil Williams was appointed to serve the church in the Tenderloin, and, like Ezekiel, faced a shattered community and a distracted congregation.

Both in and beyond the church, he walked through a valley of dry bones. Through the neighborhood were the dry bones of drug and alcohol addiction, the dry bones of selling sex for drugs, the dry bones of the hopeless and the homeless. Inside the church were the dry bones of a people who had forgotten who they were in Christ; a people who saw their task as maintaining a facility and perpetuating religious activity rather than being the living, breathing, and transforming incarnation of the Resurrected One. "Can these bones live again?" he must have wondered. And there amidst the scattered and shattered lives and the broken and dried out bones he began to speak the truth. He began to prophesy to the bones, to speak to those inside about purpose and those outside about redemption. It was a painful process, but now the church is filled beyond capacity for two services each Sunday. Outside, on the street, people wait in line to gather in the worship area and sing, pray, and hear God's story—their story—proclaimed. And beyond the powerful and diverse gathering for worship, hundreds of ministries and services aid in the process of healing and whole-making for all who would come, body and soul. The leader prophesied, the bones rose, Spirit blew and that which was dead now stands as a vast army for the Lord.

Reverend Williams, in *No Hiding Place*[2], recognized the devastating effect of spiritual amnesia and the lack of a shared story. Describing African Americans born since the civil rights struggle, especially those living in the inner city, he sees "a group lacking a sense of unifying story and connection to history. They are in the 'Diaspora' of urban struggle. They do not share a self-understanding of themselves as inheritors of the great gifts of community and faith" (Williams, p.164). When people lack connection to God's redemptive story they see themselves as isolated in a world that doesn't make sense. The goal of the church, then, becomes reaching into people's isolation and brokenness and helping them to find a new framework of meaning in the context of God's unfolding story.

One of the methods used by the congregation to provide hope and healing to such a fragmented and diverse community is to release the power of sharing stories. Addicts of all kinds, as well as people who are simply disconnected from community or God or story, gather in "Recovery circles" and share their stories. They discuss where they are and in their discussion and honesty, they end their isolation. As they share their stories, they are able to name what it is that is keeping them from being all that God has created them to be. "When the extended family gathers and by so doing answers the question of who we are as a people, incredible power is released" (Williams, p.58). Sharing of story is a source of individual and community empowerment. The leader is called to speak the story to the dry bones and help the bones find connection, healing, new life, direction, and purpose.

Shared memory and story are not only powerful for healing and for bringing life and unity to those who are broken and scattered, but they are also rich sources of purpose and direction. Memory and identity have the power to provide shared purpose and direction and continuity across time.

Church leader as baboon

I invite you to think about a story from Disney's *The Lion King,* which was a smash hit as a movie and on Broadway. The story centers on Simba, a lion cub who is destined to become the king. Simba is forced to flee his home because his evil uncle Scar convinced him that he was in some way responsible for his father's death. Simba grows up in a in the jungle far away from his home and gradually forgets that he was originally created to become king. One day, Simba has an encounter with Rafiki the baboon, a wise medicine-man character, who lures him deep into the forest by telling Simba that he knows where his father is. Simba, believing that his father is dead, is confused but intrigued and so follows the baboon through the tangled jungle to a small pool of water surrounded by high grass. Rafiki tells him to look in the pool. Simba is disappointed when all he sees is his own reflection, but Rafiki tells Simba, "*Wait... Look harder....*" With a touch of the baboon's staff, the water stirs. When the reflection comes back into focus, it is not his reflection that he sees, but the reflection of Mufasa, his father. "*You see,*" says the wise baboon, "*He lives in you.*" The image in the water then speaks to Simba and tells him, "*You have forgotten me and you have forgotten who you are.*" He reminds his son that he is destined to be so much more than what he has become. "*You must go back and take your place in the Circle of Life.*" After his encounter with his father's reflection, Simba is changed, and he heads straight back to his home to defeat Scar and take his place as king. Simba's encounter with memory transformed him and changed the direction and outcome of his life. Rafiki's role was to know the story, and to connect Simba with it in such a way that he was able to see himself. That is the role of leader as ImageSmith.

An example

In his book, *Church Leadership: Vision, Team, Culture and Integrity,*[3] Lovett Weems writes that it is important, when approaching change, to find a value or a story in the existing culture that can be lifted up as part of the process for moving into the future. Consider the following possible scenario. A leader in a congregation wants to start a new type of worship service. There is a great potential for resistance because the style of the new service seems so different from the style of the old service. Instead of approaching the task of growth and transformation with the authority of 'being right," consider the history of the congregation. Christ Episcopal Church in Kansas City faced this dilemma when planning to start a new service. The rector could have come to the people and said, "The way that you are worshiping is not reaching people of younger generations, and I know that you may be attached to these old forms of worship, but that isn't going to cut it for the new generation; therefore I have decided to start a new and different worship service that will have some life to it." That probably would have met with serious resistance. Not only would the people in the current service have felt as if their style of worship was under attack, but the unhealthy dynamic of traditional vs. contemporary would have been set up.

What the rector decided to do instead was to look to the origins of that particular church and to remember the pioneering spirit with which the founders of the church stepped out into a new and growing area and risked doing something a little different in order to reach people in the community who weren't being reached. The rector as ImageSmith touched the pool and asked them to *look harder*, and to *remember who they are*. With this approach, the congregation saw the proposed change as part of the natural process of continuing to be who they were, even if it meant offering a different style worship service. In this case, the rector was leading into the future by painting the picture of the unfolding of God's story as it had been and could be evident in the church's particular history.

Tradition and the birth of a new mission

Tradition is sometimes viewed as a negative word. It is seen as something that inhibits the leader and the congregation from moving in new and fresh ways. In many cases tradition is viewed as a series of structures that exist to be maintained for their own sake, and whose maintenance saps all the energy that should be devoted to mission. When the church becomes more interested in perpetuating the *forms of tradition* than the *purposes* that gave them birth, these assessments are accurate. Yet in another way, tradition is vital to the health of an organization, especially during times of change. The tradition to which I am referring is not the changing form, but rather the genetic code at the center of the origin of the organization. As a new mission or worship experience is launched, finding this code and remembering who we really are is just as important as looking around and asking, "who are they and what kind of service do they want?"

Many churches are experiencing aging and decline. People are asking, "Where are the young people?" One approach to reaching different generations has been to focus particular communication and worship styles to speak to each particular niche orientation. The problem with niche marketing the church for each new generation is that we lose the richness and wisdom of generational interaction. This does not mean that we never change or develop new styles of worship, but it does mean that *we must be absolutely intentional about building bridges of interaction and an attitude of shared purpose.* We are the people of God's story, not the people of this or that particular worship style. The real task is developing a culture of openness to one another and the expectation of necessary and positive change.

Once again, consider Ezekiel's method, which wasn't based on speaking to a diversity of generations, exaggerating their differences. *He communicated with them through a multi-dimensional approach that also spoke to their common experience.* His task was not niche marketing with his message to this or that particular generation of the people of God in Exile (one worship service for the aquarium dwellers, another for the aquarium visitors, and another for attracting the saltwater swimmers) but *to develop a sense of common experience that could call back into being a sense of common identity so that he could begin to paint a picture of the future that God was preparing for them.* As he was able to create a sense of shared memory and identity, the people as a group were able to develop a will to change. That group "will" enables them to move out of their fragmented life into the yet unrealized future of wholeness and hope. As they remembered, they began to see together in the present the prevenient, restored, and transformed community of God.

In my congregation, we have discovered that groups aren't merely seeking the favored music or the preferred style of communication. They are looking for authentic extended community with whom to share the journey of life, redemption, and faith. As we have grown, a multigenerational congregation has come together. There is a wide diversity of thought and perspective that gathers as part of the congregation, and there is open communication across generational lines and among people with worldviews and understandings from inside and outside the church. While a two-dimensional survey of the congregation's appearance might lead one to believe that the congregation is basically homogeneous (there is a small, yet growing ethnic minority participation), if seen on a deeper level there is tremendous diversity. People are present from all age groups, different religious and denominational backgrounds, geographic backgrounds, educational levels, socioeconomic levels, and family status. *The diversity present in the perspectives of these individuals all coming together to share in the common experience of congregation provides unique, difficult, and extremely rewarding challenges.*

In the next chapter, we will examine some of the sources of story that we need to understand and use to help connect people to God's great story.

Notes

[1] To view a color picture of the stained glass, visit www.gracehappens.org.

[2] Cecil Williams, *No Hiding Place: Empowerment and Recovery for Our Troubled Communities* (San Francisco: Harper Collins, 1992). Cecil Williams is CEO and Minister of National and International Ministries at Glide Memorial United Methodist Church in San Francisco, California.

[3] Lovett Weems, *Church Leadership: Vision, Team, Culture, and Integrity* (Nashville: Abingdon Press, 1993).

C. Bennett Bollinger

CHAPTER FOUR

Painting the Sky First: Scripture

Have you ever noticed that most young children paint or color an outdoor scene by placing everything in the foreground, and then either paint a thin blue strip of sky across the top of the page, or try to fill in with blue all around the people, trees, dogs, or other things? I love children's art and enjoy watching the creativity and spontaneity unfold, but if an accurate representation of reality is the goal, imagining the foreground first will give the viewers a distorted or immature picture. By considering a child's artwork, we learn a lesson about mature vision.

While watching my grandfather paint landscapes, I noticed that he always painted the sky first. The sky was the backdrop for the whole scene. It set the context for the world of images that would emerge on the canvas. My grandfather had a little work shed out between the big white barn and the chicken coops on his farm in Connecticut. He called the little shed his coop. He built the coop himself in which he kept most of his tools and his paints. It was filled with little drawers of tools and every type of hardware imaginable. It seemed to me that he could fix anything. Even if he didn't have the right parts for something, he would figure out a way to create something that would work. It was his workshop, office, retreat, and studio. It was there that we used to go when he would sit and pack a pipe with Liberty tobacco, strike a wooden match, and puff, puff, puff... Then he would begin to paint—anything from a still life of tulips to people in boats around a lighthouse to a beautiful countryside.

I was amazed at the way in which he would squeeze the little metal tubes, and out onto that old wooden palette would come a blob of pure color. He usually wouldn't put more than three or four colors on the palette at a time, but he knew how to blend them so that from those four or five blobs of pure color, he could create endless combinations. He knew how to layer the paints and texture them so that they would come alive on the canvas. As he combined the colors with patience, skill, creative joy, and vision, he brought forth an image of a larger reality.

Once, I sat with him in the coop and watched him start a new landscape. He worked on it for several days while I was visiting. I watched the process from beginning to end. I felt like I was witnessing creation. First, he painted the sky with broad, light strokes, filling the majority of the canvas. Next, with a smaller brush, he cut in a silhouette of the horizon; in this painting the silhouette was a background of rolling hills in fall colors. The silhouette on the horizon provided the setting for the particular scene. Later, he began to add dimension to the landscape by painting different lines of trees that seemed to be at different distances. I was amazed at the way he was able to paint with perspective. Finally, with a little putty knife and a very thin brush, he added some little flowers growing right in the foreground. They were placed right at the front edge of the scene. I felt like I wanted to step in and smell the flowers, explore the world that had just taken shape before my eyes.

Just as there are sources, various tools and different methods and techniques for painting, I believe that there are many sources of story and meaning, and a diversity of methods, tools, and techniques that the ImageSmith must draw from when trying to paint the picture of God's unfolding story.

For the ImageSmith, Scripture is the sky. Scripture forms the backdrop for all life. It sets the context for all the images that emerge in the foreground of the past, present, and future.

The backdrop of God's story

Scripture is our primary source of color and action (through story), and it reminds us of the unfolding rhythms of our lives that are part of the story of God. It reminds us that we are part of the continued cast of characters in the story of God's interaction with the world. The Bible is not just a story—it is **our** story. In these stories, we find our connection with the common themes of our life with God and God's life with us.

These are stories we must understand and dwell in intellectually and experientially. They are special stories that move us beyond an understanding of the natural world into the story of a particular people and their interaction with God. They remind us that our God did not leave creation alone to develop under its own forces and sources but rather stepped into our here-and-now to share self in revelation and love. These stories are multi-dimensional. They are the stories of the unfolding of life itself. They are stories that tell about the development of community and provide images of leadership that come from the mouth of Jesus himself. These stories connect us to the revelation of that which is beyond our natural experience, providing us with purpose and direction as we seek to move into the future that God would create through us.

Visual leaders help people learn access to the Bible

Whether we like to admit it or not, many of the people in our congregations have very little knowledge of the Bible. If Scripture is to play an important part in the formation of the lives of those we lead, it is important that we help provide tools and an environment that is conducive for learning.

The story of NOAB
and the Rainbow Bible Tabs

If we are going to help people see themselves in the stories of God, then it is important that we provide assistance for accessing the Bible. I had an experience while I was in college that made me sensitive to people who don't know their way around the Bible. I was a philosophy and theater major with an interest in the philosophy of religion. I was, at this point in my life, much more interested in thinking about religion than I was practicing it. One day I decided to go to a bible study being held by a group of students on the campus. I went because a cute, attractive girl was attending.

I showed up at the bible study with my New Oxford Annotated Bible (with Apocrypha, hereafter NOAB), they prayed, and the study began. I wasn't really paying attention to what the leader was saying. I had other things on my mind, but I noticed that they opened to the front of their Bibles, so I did too. I heard, "chapter 3, verse… something" so I looked at chapter three.

I scanned the chapter, but the words that they were reading were nothing like the words that were on my page. "What is going on?" I wondered. I glanced over to see if he had said a different chapter or something, and he looked over at my Bible. He said, "We are reading from Matthew. You are in Genesis." Then several of them started to laugh. They all had New Testaments. I had the NOAB. Now I knew something about the Bible, but it never occurred to me that someone would carry around only half of it. I laughed too, but I never went back.

I remember that moment when I stand up to preach, or when I teach a bible study, and I think of the people who are there who may not know their way around the Bible and sure don't want to pick one up and have someone notice that they don't know where to find the book of Psalms or the Gospel of John. I keep "rainbow Bible tabs" on my Bible. Rainbow Bible tabs are color-coded plastic tabs that mark the beginning of each of the books of the Bible. "Let's open Bibles to the Gospel of John, which is a little over three quarters of the way through if you have Old and New Testaments. For those of you with rainbow Bible tabs, that would be the fourth purple tab." Sometimes I joke with them: "Some people call it cheating. I call it using available technology to make the Word of God more accessible. You know, not everyone knows their way around the Bible, and that's okay here... this is a place you can learn."

One of the first priorities for a visual leader is to help members and guests understand how to read the Bible. The Bible is not simply something to be studied and dissected, and neither is it simply a resource for sermons or devotionals. The Bible is the source of our story and the beginning point of our self-understanding as the people of God. Members and guests, however, have been exposed to the Bible in many ways that leave them confused as to how to read the Bible, what to think about it, and how to understand its authority. This priority is especially important as we attempt to lead in a time when people are spiritually hungry and they are browsing at the *twenty-first century spirituality smorgasbord.*

Using Scripture to fill in the holes

Many members and guests approach the Scripture like children trying to paint the sky. The Bible isn't used as a backdrop for life or a context for our existence, but rather it is used to color in the holes or to be draped over the top, mostly out of reach. Think about some of these approaches to reading the Bible.

Some spiritual people see the Bible as an oracle. They come seeking answers to life's questions and will scan a little or use their concordance to see what a few choice Bible verses might contribute to the dilemma. While the Bible does provide direction and wisdom for living and for making decisions, the way in which we seek wisdom can cause some serious problems. Do you remember the "Magic 8-ball®"? It is a toy from the late 1960s-early 1970s, a black sphere filled with mystical-looking purple liquid and a buoyant cube with different statements on each side. The idea behind the 8-ball is that you ask it a question and then turn it over, so that the little cube floats up to the window on the bottom of the sphere. The answer that emerged was somehow the guidance you needed for that time and that place.

I remember sitting around with friends asking the 8-ball all kinds of things such as, "Does Lisa like me?" or "Will I be an astronaut?" These questions have ultimate significance about my desires and my destiny or dreams. Then, with care and effort, we would shake the ball, invert it, and peer through the glass into the mystic portal, waiting for the answers we craved... The ball always had an answer. "Absolutely," or "I wouldn't bet on it," or "Try again." The ball was reliable in that it always answered. But the answer was a roll of the dice.

I have spoken with many people who approach the Bible in this way, and who don't really know any other method. The Bible is treated as a book to consult when an answer is needed, with the hope that it will provide, by random reading, the truth or direction one seeks.

Another approach to the Scriptures that is common these days is the treatment of the Bible as if it were some sort of amulet or charm. People keep them in their houses to "keep them safe." I know of people who keep pictures of friends and loved ones in the Bible so that God will watch over them. I could understand keeping pictures of friends and loved ones in the Bible so that when I went to read, I would remember those who are close to me and I could pray for them and seek guidance and direction in our relationship, but assuming divine protection from the place-ment of photos in a book doesn't line up with the nature and purpose of Scripture.

Another approach to Scripture is found in many of the more authoritarian congregations, or in congregations that are domi-nated by a core group of Controllers. Churched people often look to Scripture for a well-defined set of boundaries. In many cases, churched people are reacting to the rapid changes taking place in the world and the overwhelming flood of information that leaves

them confused or frightened. Religious people have always grav-
itated towards a simplistic expression of faith that is clear about
who is in and who is out. It seems easier to cope with change if
"we just know who we are against, and who the enemy is."

Many members and guests look to Scripture to support what
they already believe. This circular approach does not limit itself
to uneducated people. One familiar example of this approach to
Scripture is found in the Deism of Thomas Jefferson. Jefferson
took the view that the Bible had some good things in it, but there
were many things that were primitive and superstitious. He
therefore took it upon himself to edit out the things that were
wrong and keep only the things that fit with his approach to and
his understanding of life. We don't dare lampoon this approach
too severely, because to a certain extent we each bring a set of
lenses for interpretation of the Scripture. Our reading and interpretation is always culturally biased, and we have "blind spots"
that come from our education, background, experience, and previous instruction. However, it is important that we become aware
of these tendencies so that we are shaped by Scripture rather
than shape Scripture to our own ends.

One of the most divisive issues in the Church is and has been
the problem of selective dogmatism. Selective dogmatism has to
do with finding particular social, moral, or behavioral issues, and
basing one's opinion and stance on a literal reading of that particular scripture. It is dogmatism because it develops an unwavering opinion about a particular issue or practice based on a
reading of the scripture. (Dogmas as scripturally informed beliefs
are not in and of themselves bad). The problem with selective
dogmatism is that those who practice it assume the *whole moral
authority* of the Scripture *while failing to give the same treatment
to the whole Scripture.* For example, imagine that a person takes
the position that women should not be ordained because of the
passages in Paul's writings, and defends that stance by claiming
scriptural authority. (You know—"God says it, I believe it, that
settles it...") While I don't agree with that particular interpretation of the Scripture, I see that the stance is something that can
be argued in a rational way with support from the Scripture itself.

When claiming this kind of authority for the biblical text, the implication is that the Scripture in itself is somehow authoritative. Frequently, however, people who become passionate about this or that particular issue claiming the backing of the "Word of God," ignore, belittle, or rationalize away other biblical texts with which they don't agree.

It would be easy to hold up one or two examples and to make fun of them as ignorant or shortsighted, but the truth is that for the most part, each of us practice selective dogmatism.

I naturally view history through the perspective of a white male born in a Christian home in the United States. I did not choose that perspective. Birth location happens. I can, however, work at stretching my perspective by seeking to understand cultural and historical events from a variety of perspectives. The same principle is important for the visual leader as he or she seeks to hold up the biblical story so that it becomes a unifying story and a blueprint for the Kingdom, rather than a life raft for a few.

Regardless of denomination or affiliation, we have in our communities, congregations, Sunday school classes and small groups, many people who approach the Scriptures in an immature way. It is not the task of the visual leader simply to disavow the flawed approaches and practices, and to provide appropriate study methods. Rather the visual leader will help members and guests access the story of the Scripture in ways that answer their spiritual longings. The task of the ImageSmith is to help our people paint the sky first.

Understand the tension and balance in the whole story of the Bible.

The visual leader makes use of Scripture not only as a resource for right belief and right behavior, but rather as the context of story in which we continue to live as the people of God.

At the intersection of two BIG stories

Creation

One dimension of common experience is found in the oldest of stories, which defines the rhythms of life within nature. The movement of the seasons, the complex movements of the stars and planets, the relentless tides are universally imagined as lessons about the handiwork of the creator. These are our oldest of stories. Created beings long for a connection to their source of being, and the creative and natural rhythm keeps time in and around them. This longing has led to a resurgence of interest in Native American spirituality and in the Celtic approach to spirituality. The ways in which these rhythms and stories have been expressed in New Age thought help account for the great popular interest of religious seekers in that movement.

Church leaders often shy away from the experience of the natural world. Fear of paganism and nature worship has caused Christians to avoid the spirituality of creation. The Scripture, especially in Protestant thought, appears to demand that we dominate the natural world. The Scripture advises that we are to be in but not of the world. This dualistic understanding of heaven and earth, reinforced by our living in greater separation from nature, has led our people to miss out on a deep connection with the realities of earthly spirituality. Yet Scripture itself in many ways paints a picture of a unity with the natural processes and the lessons emerging from the natural world in which we live.

A theology of creation is evident in many parts of the Scripture that helps us understand our creaturely role as tender of the garden, a part of the creation and a co-creator with God. The Scripture frequently draws imagery and wisdom from the natural world as expressions of spiritual joy or wisdom. In many cases the Scripture serves as a bridge between people and the rest of nature.

The Psalms paint pictures of creation clapping its hands:

Let the floods clap their hands;
   let the hills sing together for joy
           Psalm 98:8
   For you shall go out in joy,
     and be led back in peace;
   the mountains and the hills before you
     shall burst into song,
     and all the trees of the field shall clap their hands.
                    Isaiah 55:12

We experience in Proverbs the call to consider the ant:

Go to the ant, you lazybones;
   consider its ways, and be wise.
          Proverbs 6:6

Jesus used images of the processes of nature to teach people about the Kingdom:

> He put before them another parable: "The kingdom of heaven is like a mustard seed that someone took and sowed in his field; it is the smallest of all the seeds, but when it has grown it is the greatest of shrubs and becomes a tree, so that the birds of the air come and make nests in its branches."
>
> He told them another parable: "The kingdom of heaven is like yeast that a woman took and mixed in with three measures of flour until all of it was leavened."
>
>   Matthew 13:31-33

All of these images are opportunities for us to draw near to the world of nature and to experience and to understand. As we get so involved with the world of high tech, spectacular entertainment, and consumer-driven stories, we risk losing our footing in the rhythms of creation. As we grow to understand ourselves as dwellers in the story of creation, our relationship with the earth changes. We begin to see the presence of God more clearly and in the rhythm of nature to hear God's voice. We need to connect to that oldest story—the *earthiness* out of which we are created—if we are to lead effectively, communicate, and be fully human in this time of multiple media, multiple experience, and dwelling in fragmented, multiple stories. What would it mean for the ImageSmith to paint into the hearts and minds of the people of God an understanding of our deep, deep connectedness with the created world and to remind us that it is in that world that we see the very fingerprint of our creator God?

Howard Hangar is a jazz pianist and ordained minister in Asheville, North Carolina. He leads in our Conference Academy for Spiritual Leadership. During his time with the participants, he has us do things like go outside, take off our shoes, and feel the warmth of the sun. He talks about the four directions that surround us, and the ways in which those directions are symbols for understanding our experiences in life and faith. We turn to the North—the source of the cold wind—and become aware of those times in our lives that are filled with difficulty. To the South—the place of the warm breezes—he remembers comfort, rest, home, family, and love. We turn to the East and recall the sunrise—the place of new beginnings and are reminded that God is the giver of life and that God continually makes all things new. We are reminded of the resurrection of Christ and the new life that is given for each one of us. We turn to the West, and as the setting sun turns the sky orange and purple, we are reminded that each of us will have an end to our days, that there are always beginnings and endings and that God is there as well, ready to receive us into open arms. Inviting us to follow his motions, we join in a prayer:

> With the whole earth, You feed my soul,
> With all the creatures of the earth, You feed my soul,
> With the wind and the rain, You feed my soul,
> With the stars in the heavens, You feed my soul,
> And I grow strong, in heart and mind, with Your food.
> Thank You.[1]

As we stand there in the soft breeze of the warm May evening, listening to the birds and feeling the grass beneath our feet, we feel close to one another and close to God. Howard paints the picture of the story of the Creator God in a way that attaches the truth of the Scripture with the reality of our common human experience—and we understand... *ImageSmith.*

Understanding creation as part of our story is extremely important for leaders of congregations today, especially as our world becomes more high-tech, high speed, and media driven. People are separated from the natural world and can easily forget that they are part of the process and interplay of God's creation. Theologian Matthew Fox lifts up the need for what he calls *Creation Spirituality.*[2] Creation spirituality is a way of interpreting who we are as the children of God, as people who are part of creation. It is a spirituality that helps us to understand the basis for caring for all life and protecting the earth. It is a spirituality that helps us see the importance and beauty of life on earth instead of focusing so much on the afterlife. As an ImageSmith I am drawn toward a creation-based spirituality, if it is not proposed as the only lens for God's work in the world. When Matthew Fox calls, however, for a creation spirituality to *replace* our theology based on redemption, he ignores the evidence that God is at work in our histories. To chose one dimension of scriptural identity over another as a basis for all theological reflection and understanding is to miss the richness of the biblical story. We are both *created ones* and *redeemed ones.* God is our Redeemer too.

Redemption

The second BIG dimension of the story in which we live is God's activity of redemption. We are part of a world of brokenness and sin. We are part of a world of violence and oppression, hunger, and pain. The Scripture is filled with examples of broken people and the broken societies that they inhabit. Our newspapers, TV channels, and feature films are filled with stories and images of broken individuals and the broken societies we inhabit. This similarity between the bible stories and the human story is the very basis of our appreciation of Scripture. The good news of the faith in light of the brokenness and sinfulness of our world is that while we are part of a world that is fallen, we have not been abandoned. That same caring creator God who brought all of this into being in the first place, could have designed creation like an Etch A Sketch,® given it a good shake, and started over. Instead, the creator took the form of a human and came to dwell with us in our midst. God came in Christ to atone for the world's sins, and to make available to all people the gift of grace, forgiveness, another chance, and a new beginning.

I am amazed when I talk with individuals about the concept of grace. As many churches as there are, and as long as this doctrine has been taught, it still seems that churched people have an understanding that God's grace and love are *beliefs to be held rather than descriptions of the reality (discerned in stories) in which we live and breathe and have our hope.* Scripture helps paint the order of salvation so that people can see themselves in the scene.

What is original sin? How does that relate to me? How is Jesus the answer to the problems of my life?

Many people think about sin as if sin were some sort of activity. If I am a sinner, it means that I am sinning. Sinning is defined as a set of behaviors that are not approved by Scripture or society— "Don't drink, don't smoke, don't chew, don't go with girls who do." What about looking at the backdrop of Scripture in order to see the concept of sin as part of our condition rather than a set of behaviors to avoid? In the story of the Garden of Eden, in many instances, sin is seen as the eating of the apple. The act of disobedience was the sin.

Think again: Eating the apple was a symptom of a shift in perspective and orientation.

The situation in the garden prior to the apple event was one of freedom to do and to be in a playground of possibility and beauty. The story centered in God and likewise was the mind of the individual centered in relationship with the God. The serpent entered the situation and turned the focus from being God-centered to being self-centered. That shift away from God and toward the self precedes the "*crunch.*" Sin is not the act of disobedience, but rather disobedience emerges from the self-centered perspective.

I've heard acquaintances say, "I don't believe in original sin. If you have ever looked at a baby, how can you believe in original sin? They haven't done anything wrong. They are beautiful little gifts from God."

Do you hear the understanding of the nature of sin implicit in the question? Sin is seen as something that is done. *The baby hasn't sinned—yet.* What changes when the concept of sin is reframed to reflect not the act of disobedience, but rather the perspective of self-centeredness? When babies are hungry, they don't usually say, "Let me begin by expressing my appreciation for the gift of life. Without you I would be nothing. Thanks as well for the love you have for me and the home you are providing. You have given me shelter and a place to lay my head. Thanks for being my parents. Now, I know that you are extremely busy, and that there are many important things you need to be doing, but when you get a moment, would you mind terribly bringing me something to eat?" Babies demonstrate a different perspective. Their internal dialogue might run more along the lines of, "I am hungry. I want food. Feed me now. And what is this stuff in my diaper? Can't you tell that I am uncomfortable? Change me now! ME NOW! ME NOW!" Some adults never move beyond this perspective.

The activities associated with sinning are the result of the attitude of self-centeredness rather than God-centeredness. It is into this context that Christ the Redeemer, the Savior, enters our world.

Look back at the entrance that Christ made and think about the meaning of redemption in that context. Think about those shepherds out there in the field. They hear the angel's message and then they have to figure out what that means. "A savior—for us—hmmm…" What is a savior for a shepherd? They were not sitting around thinking, "Oh no, without a savior, I'm doomed to burn in hell for all eternity." The fear of hell was not part of the discussion at this point. They had an understanding that if they were living with God in this life, then they would continue to live with God—for what would separate them?

So, what would a savior be for a shepherd? A savior from... wolves, from boredom, from the fragrance of the gentleman sitting next to you? Angels came right into the midst of their lives and said, "a savior for you." What does that mean?

If you are in a well, a deep well, can't touch the bottom and the sides are mossy and slippery, and it's cold, and there's nobody around, and all you can do is tread water until you get so tired you are going to faint. What would a savior be? A savior would be someone with a rope who could drop it down, loop it around you, give you hope in a situation where there was no hope, and give you passage out of that place that was threatening your life.

If you're wandering around blindfolded on the edge of a cliff in the dark by yourself, what would a savior be? Someone to grab you, stop you, take the blindfold off, and lead you away from there so you don't go falling off the cliff—that would be a savior.

If you smelled like sheep so that others mocked you or at least didn't want to be around you and you lived in a field with other men, what would a savior be? Maybe it would be someone who said, "I know you are there. I haven't forgotten you. Even though you sleep outside on the outskirts of town and you smell bad, I care for you and I'll never leave you alone."

If you were living in a society that was being oppressed by an outside government, what would a savior be? A savior would be the Messiah who would come to liberate the people and bring in the reign of God.

If you were living in a world that was telling you that what you've got to do is make more money, do more, and buy more stuff, what would a savior be? If you were living in a world that was telling you that you can find meaning by developing particular lifestyles and wearing brand names, what would a savior be? If you were living in a world that told you that it's all about you and what matters is looking out for number one, what would a savior be? Perhaps it would be someone who could reach in and show you again the whole and holy nature of the gift of life that God has given to each one of us.

Of course, salvation does pertain to eternal life. God came for that reason. Jesus was sent into the world for that reason—that our lives might be restored and we might have eternity with God. But if God had merely wanted our eternal souls, God could have either said, "I'm not creating life, they're just going to mess up. I'm just going to keep a bunch of souls eternally; beautiful nice little souls." That view would have made sense if "souls" are the desired outcome, would it not?

Or, God could have said, "Oops, they've all messed up" But instead of sending a child down to earth to die, (so the people have to make a choice as to where they end up and then ending up with *only some of the souls*) God could just say, "All right, anytime they die, their soul is coming up. I'm going to bring them into perfect peace with me for eternity. That takes care of it, does it not? My desire is to save souls and pull them all up here to be in peace with me for eternity, so they're coming up, and we'd better get the party started." But, God didn't do that.

God saw the value of *this life here and now*—the beauty and the gift of this life here and now—and wanted not just to redeem an eternal soul but to redeem life itself; to redeem creation, individuals, and society. God is present with us, here and now as designer of creation and redeemer of our individual stories.

God cared enough to come to people who sat on the isolated edges of life in the darkness with sheep in order to enter into their lives. It is the same God who enters into the present-time of our lives. The same God says to each of us, "For you, this day, a Savior." The same God who has given us life, in all of its fullness comes to us again. Our here and now is redeemed and our future is filled with hope because of the transforming hand of God. You see it's there. It is the backdrop of our lives. God's gift of grace awaits our response, and when we step into that life and say "Yes, take me!" we not only are forgiven and reoriented, but we get to be story agents of God's life and light in the world

Jesus was asked "What is the greatest commandment?" He replied, "Love the Lord your God with all your heart, soul, and mind, and love your neighbor as yourself." This commandment is an expression of the original intention for human life as represented in the garden. What were humans created to do? They were created to love the Lord with all their heart, soul, and mind and to love their neighbor as their own being.

> So if anyone is in Christ, there is a new creation: everything old has passed away; see, everything has become new! All this is from God, who reconciled us to himself through Christ, and has given us the ministry of reconciliation; that is, in Christ God was reconciling the world to himself, not counting their trespasses against them, and entrusting the message of reconciliation to us. So we are ambassadors for Christ, since God is making his appeal through us; we entreat you on behalf of Christ, be reconciled to God. (2 Corinthians 5:17-20)

The ministry of reconciliation has been given to us. We are the created ones. We are the redeemed ones, and we are storytellers of the new creation.

We live at the intersection of two BIG stories—where heaven touches earth—against the backdrop of the Grace of the Creator, Redeemer, and Sustainer God. The task of the ImageSmith is to help the people paint the sky first so that they will become a community of people who understand the story in which they live and are able to share it with others in word and action. The purpose of the Scripture is to build the community of those who dwell in God's story and tell God's story as they go about increasing love of God and neighbor.

Notes

[1] Howard Hangar at www.howardhangar.com and www.jubileecommunity.org.

[2] Matthew Fox, *Creation Spirituality: Liberating Gifts for the Peoples of the Earth* (San Francisco: Harper Collins, 1991).

C.BennettBollinger

CHAPTER FIVE

Silhouetting the Horizon: Tradition

After painting the sky and preparing the backdrop for the emerging world of images, my grandfather would take a slightly smaller brush and silhouette the horizon. He envisioned a distant firmament that is under the sky, but still behind all the other images that would emerge. Sometimes the horizon would be composed of trees or mountains; sometimes clouds, or the distant edge of the sea. The silhouette of the horizon provided the particular setting for the scene. For the ImageSmith, set against the backdrop of Scripture, is the silhouetted horizon of tradition. The tradition and history that stand behind the foreground of our lives provide a setting and direction for the emerging images of our life and ministry.

I wonder

While in high school I was in a production of "Fiddler on the Roof." I remember, at the time hearing Tevye speak the words, *"Without tradition, life would be as shaky as a fiddler on the roof,"* and wondering what it would be like to live in a time of such great change; a where one set of deeply held traditions was being challenged by a rapidly changing world. I wondered what it would be like to be part of a family that struggled with holding on to the value of tradition without being overwhelmed by the world. This is such a difficult struggle: parents and grandparents holding faithfully to time-honored, deeply rooted, and meaning-

79

ful traditions, while the children wrestle with being faithful to family and heritage as they live and find new love in a radically changed world. I wondered about this as a youth, but I have arrived like you at the conclusion that we live with that tension between tradition and new experiences. Given enough maturity, we can see that this tension has always existed, whether precipitated by war or economic conflict or religious exclusivity.

This tension and conflict between tradition and change is felt in powerful ways in our churches. Many churches are paralyzed in internal conflict between polarizing groups who seem to be competing for power, control, or authority. On one side, we may align with those who stand for maintaining the integrity of tradition, and on the other side, we may align with those who want to risk doing new things to reach new people for God. During periods of polarizing conflict, the ImageSmith must have a grasp on the realities of tradition in order to help the different factions of any given community of faith find elements of common ground and shared story.

€state litigation

The present-day struggles in many congregations have taken on the flavor of estate litigation. One of the most painful sights is to see members of the same family tearing at the very fabric of who they are and who they might become in order to lay claim to certain pieces of the family property. I have seen, on numerous occasions, people changed for the worse and entire families destroyed and embittered during such struggles. Many times the struggle for the *stuff* is really a struggle for the *title* of "Mom or Daddy's favorite." A family that existed to build love, unity, and provide stability in the storms of life becomes a place of anger and division. Those who gathered around the table to pray and eat and share nourishment and story now argue about whose table it is and who has the right to decide what happens to it.

The problem in some churches is found with one group that passionately believes that faithfulness means upholding the tradition and heritage that has been given to them. Faithfulness means protecting the sacred traditions and practices from those who are easily swayed by cultural change and too ready to "sell out" for the sake of numbers. Another group believes just as passionately that in order to hold on to the purpose and mission of the church, it is necessary to communicate and worship in different ways. For this group faithfulness means rescuing the mission of the church from the tomb of inward focus and the practice of lifeless ritual. Ouch. Maintaining lifeless ritual. Ouch! Selling out the tradition for the sake of numbers. What hurtful words are these? If we continue to see our situation as a war between two groups (one faithful, and the other unfaithful, changing according to the position one holds), we will, as a church family, use up all the energy that ought to be directed toward a more collaborative mission.

What if there was a way to reframe this conflict so that both "sides" could see themselves working toward a common goal for a common cause rather than against each other? Rather than embracing tradition as something that must be maintained, or rejecting tradition as something that must be jettisoned, perhaps we might look at the situation in a different way. Visual leaders see past this polarization by learning to understand tradition and to add stories to the mix of our congregation's memory matrix, not dogmatically or obtrusively, but rather gently, warmly, as if sharing pictures of one's family. In the sharing of these memories, we find ground for shared life and shared direction.

Tradition as faded family photographs

My mind flashes back to the farm in Connecticut where my family spent part of each summer during my childhood. On this particular occasion, however, I return not only as grandson but as ordained minister. I am asked to conduct my grandmother's funeral. It is a difficult thing to do, but the process of preparing that funeral draws me deeply into an exploration of my own memories of my grandmother and all of the strands of history, memory, and emotion that are part of the experience.

After the funeral, everyone has gone home, then my aunt shares with me an album of pictures that provides many new strands of memory. There are pictures of all of my mother's family while they were growing up. There are pictures of places and people—relatives—some I've never met. Yet in the simple act of gazing at these faded photographs, and sharing their story, I enter into a part of my life that I have never known before. I drink from a well of memory from which my soul can draw identity and richness, which has before been covered over by time and distance. The silhouettes on the horizon of my life become clearer.

In one sense, the journey into the world of these faded photographs is a nostalgic trek into a bygone era, yet in another way it is an important opportunity for me to explore the landscape of my history, and to be stretched into a deeper awareness of the connection of the passage of time and the fleetingness of life.

Just as you are awakened to a part of your own being in the exploration of an immediate family history, so too can we as the children of God find a new source of story, shared memory, and common identity in our history and our tradition. In the exploration of our history we gain access to a new richness from which to draw as we describe the world in which we live and move.

Tradition, like an old faded photograph, is the story of our historical experience as people of God through history, liturgy, and the development of congregation, community, and culture. Through tradition and history, we understand better our predecessor's experience of family, community, and leadership.

Playing on the grave

I grew up in the home of an historian who specialized in understanding the contributions of the Wesleys to Methodism. In sixth grade I lived near Oxford, England. I was not too happy about leaving my friends at the time, but by looking back, I can see that this time in a different country was one of the ways that God was shaping me for ministry. My parents carted my brother and me all around England and parts of Europe to see castles and cathedrals, culture and countryside, museums and art galleries.

As a little boy, I heard the stories of the history of the Christian church and especially the origins of the Methodist movement as I saw the places where it began.

I remember climbing and playing on the big old stone grave of Samuel Wesley (John Wesley's father) in the churchyard at St. Andrews parish church in Epworth. This was the parish in which John Wesley grew up and experienced baptism, communion, congregational life, and liturgy. It was at this church that John and his brother Charles learned about Jesus and his concern for the lost and the poor. It was here that he learned the stories from the Book of Acts about the church that met in the temple as well as in the homes of the believers. It was here that he learned of the radical commitment of the disciples who responded to Jesus' words, "follow me," and the way in which those disciples were sent into "the world to make disciples of all nations."

John's father, Samuel, was the Anglican priest of this parish until his death, and, as a long-tenured minister, was buried in a large stone grave close to the entrance of the sanctuary and fully aboveground. After becoming a "field preacher" in order to reach out to thousands of people, John Wesley returned to St. Andrew's for a visit, but because of his reputation, the new rector at his father's church would not allow him to preach. John went outside, climbed atop his father's grave and preached. I climbed on that grave as a child.

I saw the church he built in London and the little room in his house next door that was the place where he prayed every morning. In Oxford, I visited the college where he became part of the Holy Club and developed the disciplines and practices that led to the group label, "Methodist." I stood in the pulpit of the first Methodist meeting house ever built, which was used for preaching and the training of preachers. I walked in the room that was at once sanctuary, meeting room, training center, medical clinic, pharmacy, and recovery center. I ran and kicked the soccer ball in the fields where John Wesley preached to thousands of uneducated, impoverished coal miners who felt separated from the existing church, but who responded to and were transformed by a Gospel that came to them.

These stories are embedded into my coming of age, and for some reason, I assumed that everyone else knew them as well. After I started serving the church as a pastor, I discovered that most people don't know the stories. They haven't seen the family photos. They see the *forms* of tradition but don't know the *heart*, the *lungs*—the embodied *story*.

Sharing the scrapbook

Several people in our congregation are really into *scrapbooking*. They get together and have parties to cut out pictures and put together memorabilia into scrapbooks. In your congregation there are probably also persons who become engrossed in genealogy, in excavating and explaining the memory of their ancestors. At first we wonder about the amount of time and money that some people spend on making scrapbooks or ancestral charts, but then we realize that they are rehearsing the memories that are meaningful to them, and putting them in a form, a type of genetic code that could be passed down to the next generation and the next. They want the richness of the memory of family and life to be shared with those who are yet to come. Instead of finding boxes of envelopes that are filled with photos but with no explanation, and no point of reference or context, they want to perpetuate the memories in the context of story and make them accessible to others. These DNA memories help them make sense of who they are and where they fit in the currents of our culture.

As I became aware of so many congregations becoming caught in "estate litigation" over the tradition and mission of the church, I perceived an opportunity for sharing of the scrapbook. I often share the experiences and stories of our ancestors, which I have been privileged to hear within the context where they emerged. In these stories is a dimension of life that is being missed when plundering the estate. This desire to decipher our DNA inspired the creation of the ReConnecting video series. It is a "scrapbook" filled in seven parts with family memories. Through this scrapbook we can bring the experience and the stories of the origins of the Methodist Movement to people who haven't yet heard.

To retrace these origins, I and a videographer in my church and our spouses formed a team and went to England to film. As we went from London to Oxford to Bristol to Epworth, and so on, I felt a sense of adventure in developing a closer connection with the past. The journey to England with the purpose of remembering and translating the stories of our Wesleyan heritage kindled in me a living sense of connection to the heritage that had already been mine. I had read the history and I had been to the historic locations before. They had been an important part of my spiritual formation, but something was different this time. Touching the past rekindled my own childhood spiritual experiences, but the creative task of telling the stories caused me to feel as if I were walking with that *"great cloud of witnesses"* in Hebrews, along with those who have since then entered into their presence. As I walked they were saying, *"Remember..."*

Our film is now published as one of seven video sessions in *Reconnecting: A Wesleyan Guide for the Renewal of Our Congregation* (Abingdon Press, 2002).[1]

Listening to the stories at the center of our tradition extended the roots of my experience into a time before my existence, and that experience has deepened my passion for and appreciation of our purpose and mission. Helping those in our congregations to access these stories of tradition can have a profound effect.

Adding tradition to our color palette

By adding the dimension of tradition and history to the DNA of our congregation, we rekindled some exciting developments. Over 300 people signed up to participate in the seven-week experience of *ReConnecting*. As the participants watched video sessions, read from Wesley's words and the scriptures, and shared their reflections together, things began to happen. I listened to conversations as the weeks passed.

During the fourth week of the study, the group was exploring Wesley's outreach center in Bristol. It was a building designed to house various activities of ministry such as feeding the poor, providing medical care, teaching job skills, and training ministry leaders. One of the groups included a Realtor. She was usually very quiet and seemed somewhat reserved. After the session she called me. She had been thinking about the origins of the church and about our church's growing need for more space. She'd been praying about ways that we could be in ministry with those in the community, much like the approach at the New Room in Bristol. She was aware of an old hotel downtown that had been available for quite some time, and she thought that it might meet the needs for more space and community outreach. So we went to look at a hotel. More people became interested, and soon there was a entire group discussing more space and an outreach center. After several tours, discussions with architects and the EPA, we ruled out the old hotel (too much asbestos) but the story of the New Room had given birth to an idea.

We became aware that a church in a "high need" part of town was closing because most of the twenty-five people who remained were seventy or older, no longer lived in the neighborhood, and just couldn't keep it going any more. We realized that everyone else was looking to get out of the neighborhood, and we were looking for a way to get into the area. We began discussions with the Conference, and we were given the church building to use as a center for ministries such as feeding the poor, providing medical care, teaching job skills, and training ministry leaders. Several of us gathered in the chancel area of the old church building to consider what God might do there. We prayed. I read the passage about the bones coming to life. We looked around and listened for God's dream in that place. Before long, people from the congregation flocked to the facility to clean and prepare it for its rebirth in ministry.

In the first summer of its existence, the new facility became the home of a theater troupe made up of youth from four different groups: the Juvenile Department of Corrections, a residential facility for homeless families, the African American congregation with whom we are in partnership, and the congregation I serve. The participants spent the summer with mentors, leaders, and artists learning and working together to share their own stories and to produce a play entitled "This Is Who I Am." Our Director of Missions and Community Involvement developed and directed the production. Through participation in the event, the youth began to see beyond traditional boundaries that had separated them. They built bridges of understanding that will serve them well as they grow to become leaders. The new facility also made way for the birth of a free medical clinic, helping to heal people, body and soul. A place that had been struggling to hold on was reborn to foster the development of creativity, redemption, and healing. The name of the facility is *The New Room*, named after the first Methodist building ever built. Why? Because our identity has been colored by an understanding of who we have been and the roots of tradition from which we spring.

The connection with history has provided the congregation with a depth that was not present previously because we were a congregation that had only a few years of experience and history together. Now, instead of being a congregation that shares a common memory that stretches back only a few years, we know the Wesley stories as if they were our own. We share the understanding of being Christians in a time of great social change. We understand our purpose to reach out beyond the walls and touch lives being missed by the standard ways of doing church. We are fortified by the courage of our Methodist ancestors as we face stepping out into new forms of ministry and new areas of need. "If our Methodist ancestors did it, then we can too." New energy and unity came from imagining the stories of our heritage, by sharing the scrapbook. This is visual leadership in connection with that old, old story and the unfolding of God's light in the people of God throughout the ages.

This healthy respect for tradition is not merely something that can emerge only in a new church. In fact, most new churches started in the past twenty-five years, and motivated in part by distrust of ineffective bureaucracies, have made a conscious claim of avoiding seemingly tired traditions that are drawn from aging denominations. However, drawing leadership energy from the stories and experiences of our respective traditions is a workable transformation that is appropriate to many settings. The process of *ReConnecting* found a powerful response when used in a very old, historic center-city church in rural Louisiana. The pastor saw the struggle and the tension between those who declared themselves as the keepers of tradition and those who wanted to reach out in new ways to the changing culture around them. The pastor saw the tension between the groups that was sapping the energy from the leaders and from his ministry. In order to help the church refocus so they could move forward in ministry, it was necessary to provide the members of the congregation with a shared experience that would reframe their situation and give them a new perspective on their task. He knew how important tradition is to this congregation, and he also knew that surrounding them, as in the days of Wesley, were large numbers of people who were not being reached. He understood that being faithful to Wesleyan tradition meant reaching out beyond the walls and forms of the church to touch people where they were.

The leadership set out to draw as many people as possible at the center-city church into a shared memory. They decided to focus on this one experience as the priority for the congregation. Through newsletter articles, announcements, and sermons, the congregation was informed about and encouraged to participate in the journey. Groups were offered at a variety of times to provide maximum accessibility for members of the congregation with diverse and busy schedules. Over 150 people signed up and participated in the experience.

Later the pastor shared the following results that emerged from their shared experience:

❖ Eight new individuals/couples signed up for small group leader training.

❖ Six participants formed a task group to develop a new series of adult education opportunities to accompany the new worship service.

❖ Twenty participants expressed interest in participating in the new educational opportunities.

❖ A visioning taskforce was established to discern vision and direction for the church.

❖ Fifteen participants requested a program to help them understand ministry according to spiritual gifts.

❖ Eighteen participants registered for DISCIPLE *Bible Study.*

❖ Twenty-two participants registered for a spiritual growth group.

❖ A group was formed to assess what was necessary to facilitate developing ministries that would reach more . effectively beyond the walls of the church.

❖ Interest was expressed in exploring the possibility of developing a second site for the church to enable more people to be reached and the church to grow in ministry, mission, and members.

Many popular leadership books hold that tradition is a negative force, binding the leader to the past in addictive and unhealthy practices. Sometimes individuals do have an unhealthy attraction to the past. Defending the tradition sometimes cloaks personal self-interest. At times, traditional practices stand in the way of innovation. However, it is neither the past nor the tradition that is inherently faulty. Rather it is more likely that interpersonal conflict is framing the perspective of past, present, and future in the wrong way. Mission-driven vision, direction, and energy are found in the primal stories of our respective traditions, because they provided indispensable energy for the rebirthing of mission. Adding tradition to the canvas brought forth renewed energy and has engendered a rebirth of passion that launched the movement (Methodist in my setting) into ministry from the very beginning. Becoming a slave to the forms of tradition, or perpetuating theological conflicts that are no longer decisive, can stagnate organization and stifle visionary leaders, but adding tradition to the palette of the ImageSmith can add a source inspiration that will change the future of your ministry.

Tradition in transition

This is a difficult and important time as the church struggles to be faithful and effective in a rapidly changing world. There are great pressures and tensions from both inside and outside the congregations. Many leadership books refer to our predicament as an "in-between" time. As the world continues to change, many are developing new forms of worship and ministry in an attempt to be relevant to the changing culture. Michael Slaughter of Ginghamsburg Church (a United Methodist congregation) observes in *UnLearning Church* [2] that God is doing new things all over the church. However, rather than a bunch of McChurch franchises that form yet another bureaucracy, he pleads for an openness in each congregation to pursue what God is calling for this particular cultural situation. Pastor Slaughter reminds us to avoid duplicating the forms of religion that make no sense to new generations of believers, but in trying to stay relevant he also recognizes a danger in embracing change so quickly that one cannot manage or implement the vision. Even while God is doing a new thing for a new day, this doesn't mean that we remove the tradition from our color palette of leadership.

Many years after graduating from seminary, I was sitting in my living room one evening when the phone rang. On the other end of the line was one of my favorite professors. He was calling to tell me that he was getting married. His wife of many years had passed away and after some time of grieving, he rediscovered a friendship from an earlier time in his life and over time fell in love. I congratulated him and asked for the date so I could come and celebrate the event with him and his fiancé. Then came the story of his pastor who was recovering from some very serious surgery and most likely wouldn't be able to perform the wedding. He told me that his daughter was in seminary and would like to assist in the service, and he asked me to perform the ceremony if his pastor was not recovered in time. I was honored to be asked and assured him that I would be there, and would officiate if needed.

Because I was traveling by plane, I planned to borrow a robe for the service, and the professor asked if I would like to wear his. I agreed. As the service was about to begin, standing in the hall, I put on the white robe. It was a flowing white silk chasible. It felt a little different from the robes I had worn, but I liked it. The time came for us to process into the church. I took my place in line and made my way to the front of the church. The music was beautiful and filled the huge, vaulted sanctuary.

As the music came to a close, we stood—the gathering of community in a place of sacred memory. Almost by autopilot I stepped up to begin the service. While looking out over the faces of the congregation, I saw familiar faces. I saw professors with whom I had studied history, theology, Scripture, and ethics. I saw the bridegroom standing in a tuxedo preparing to be married. I saw my parents, who had come to celebrate the occasion because they had been friends of the professor for almost fifty years. He and my father had been students in the Wesley Foundation together in college. I saw the stained glass windows that told stories of the events of the Bible refracting light and washing the congregation with their colors. I saw the Bible and the hymnal containing Word, liturgy, and song—*these elements of tradition were in my hands.*

I felt the robe. I felt the weight of that white silk robe, and I realized what was happening. I was not just wearing my professor's robe. I had taken on the mantle of the *story*—the *tradition* and the *richness of our shared history and mission.* I was overwhelmed with a sense of responsibility, which an egocentric leader might confuse with authority. I could feel the lump rising in my throat and my eyes welling up with tears. The tears came. I shared with the congregation what I had just witnessed, and there, bathed in the richness of tradition, we shared in the making of a new covenant that would shape lives into the future.

Living tradition is a powerful thing. It is a rich source of color for the leader, and a rich source of identity for the body of Christ. We hold onto tradition neither to idolize the past nor legitimate personal power, but to lead the community to see itself in the landscape of our predecessors, among a cloud of witnesses who sit above the horizon. Scripture and tradition are the sources of story and guidance passed on to us from the cloud of witnesses who have passed this way before. Reason and experience are ways in which we receive and interpret life in relation to these sources of color. In the following two chapters, we will examine the importance of both reason and experience, the limits of each separately, and the necessity of holding the two in creative tension.

Notes

[1] "Reconnecting" is a seven-week video and journaling based process designed to facilitate a journey of exploration and discovery into a deeper connectedness with our Wesleyan heritage, vision, spirituality, leadership.

Over the course of the seven weeks, those who participate will look first-hand at some of the biggest challenges and opportunities facing the church. Together they take a video journey to England in order to remember the stories of our origins. Through video sessions and daily readings, participants visit with outstanding theologians, church leaders, and congregations. Through journaling, prayer, and group discussion, they establish those connections within their hearts and groups as well.

Those who participate in the study will view a video weekly and use workbooks to guide them through a journey of learning and discovery that can help churches grow and move forward in a time of changes and choices. It will help participants see the need not only to sustain but also to reenergize the church as it seeks to be faithful to its mission of making disciples "in Jerusalem, and in all Judea and Samaria, and to the ends of the earth," even if that means speaking a different language across generational lines.

[2] Michael Slaughter, *Unlearning Church: Just When You Thought You Had Church All Figured Out!* (Loveland: Group Publishing, 2001).

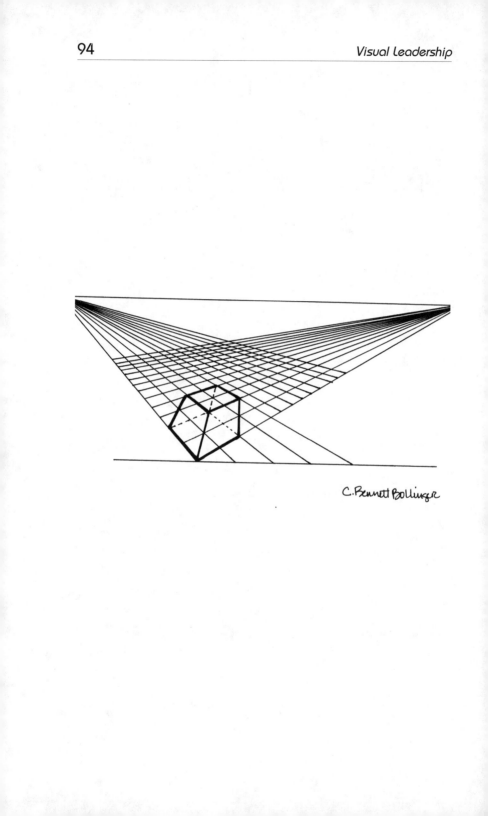

C. Bennett Bollinger

CHAPTER SIX

Painting with Perspective: Reason

A fter establishing the background and the silhouetted horizon, the amazing phase began. He began to make the two-dimensional canvas take on a third dimension. It stunned me to see how he was able to make some things look like they were right there and some things look like they were fifty yards away. I would try to do the same thing, but my drawings never looked the same. It wasn't until much later that I began to understand the mechanical process behind the creation of the third dimension.

While in college, one of my majors was theater. As part of the requirements, I took a course in set design. We learned to draw and paint in perspective. Perspective painting was the innovation of Leonardo DaVinci. He developed a grid based on geometry and spatial relationships. Perspective painting enables the artist/designer to design a stage in three dimensions, keeping things in right relation to each other. By adding reason in the application of colors from the palate of the ImageSmith, the leader learns (through much practice) to paint with perspective. The leader moves beyond narrowness and one-dimensional thinking into depth and complexity. Reason provides the tools for figuring things out, making comparisons, analyzing contradictions, highlighting emphases, and resolving problems.

Compartmentalization and the closing of the mind

One person who came to visit our church told me of something that she experienced which had disturbed her deeply. She was attending another church. She had supportive friends and enjoyed the fellowship, but recently there had been a big brouha-ha about the creation vs. evolution controversy. It seems that her pastor was passionate about this doctrinal conflict, so he preached a sermon on *faith in the face of science*. In that sermon, based on his reading of the Scriptures, he attempted to explain away all of the scientific claims about evolution.

One of his points caused her to question his approach. He stated that the age of the earth could be traced back through the ages of people found in the pages of the Scriptures, all the way back through the seven days of creation. He concluded that the earth was a little less than 7,000 years old. This seemed to be a logical argument, and as such would be a solid basis for drawing some conclusions about the mistakes of modern science. If the earth is only 7,000 years old, "as the Scripture proves," then the reports of the scientists are simply wrong about the earth being billions of years old. As for the dinosaurs, he went on to report, their bones have been placed in the soil and the rocks, to serve as a test of our faith and of our strict adherence to the truth of the Scripture.

Church leaders frequently use reason to support a hardened "biblical" perspective. In this case the preacher is not simply pitting biblical literalism against reason or science. When he explains the origins of the dinosaur bones and tracks as "placed there by God as a test" he is going beyond Scripture (which offers no basis for this claim) to give a *reasonable explanation*. In the appeal to reason, we must be able to offer evidence to support our claims. If some of the evidence contradicts our claim, or if the evidence is absent, we take an educated guess. In the church, our guesses are often given the same authority as Scripture. However, reasonable thinkers will avoid absolute conclusions and hold their opinions graciously until more evidence is available. Educated guesswork happens in science too, which is one reason why polarizing conflict emerges among church leaders and preachers who see the Bible and the world as if there are only black and white colors.

Fish wars

On another level, we see this polarizing conflict being played out by little chrome symbols that people place on their cars. I'm sure you have seen the little fish that people put on their cars to express their faith in Christ. Those fish became very popular and soon they began to evolve into more complex symbols. Some of the fish were simple line drawings; next came the fish that was filled with the word "ichthus" (fish) which stands for the phrase "Jesus Christ the Savior is Lord." Perhaps this wasn't clear enough, so then came the chrome fish with the word Jesus spelled in it. The symbolic metal trend is an interesting development in the act of witnessing. No longer do unbelievers look to see if we are Christians because of our love. Instead, all the losers need to do is to look at the back of the car. But the battle of symbolism isn't over yet. As the chrome Christian fish gained popularity, and the debate over creation vs. evolution loomed large in the school boards around the country, another fish made its way onto the hind-end of cars. This time the fish has feet.

Evolving along the same lines as the previous generation of fish, to the fish with feet is added the word *Darwin*. The symbol of the Christian fish is taken over by the fish with feet to represent the process of evolution. Some Christians are outraged. Anger rises up in them as they see the depiction of Darwinism on the backside of cars. What is this world where people of reason mock people of faith?

Someone decided that it is time to strike back for Christ and for Creationism, so they created yet another fish emblem. This time, it is a Christian fish with an attitude. The new symbol shows a larger Jesus fish that is eating the smaller, footed, Darwin fish. Yes! That should do it. That should show the heathen what is right and true!

In this fish war neither side really wants to engage the argument or the position of the other. They just fight. Reason (understood as a symbol) is deployed as a weapon, and thus cannot open doors to any kind of new understanding, especially one that might draw reasonable persons to Christ.

The visitor who came to me about the dinosaurs was not schooled in theological argument, and she wasn't looking for an explanation of how it is that dinosaurs fit into the picture of faith. That wasn't the issue for her. There was some sort of an existential discontinuity that was causing her to struggle with the validity of a faith that would claim such a strange and narrow interpretation of reality. How can this situation be reframed in order to provide us with a more productive discussion that changes people's lives? It is the task of the ImageSmith to *paint with perspective* and help people see a larger reality in which faith isn't "at war" with science.

The movie, *Inherit the Wind*, is about the Scopes Monkey Trial that began on July 10, 1925. It was a trial involving a biology teacher who was teaching modern science and referring to evolution in the classroom. Some church people became furious and tried to force him to stop teaching the "doctrine of evolution" because it was against the law to teach the subject in the state of Tennessee. The movie centers on the arguments by the two lawyers, one representing the position of the state of Tennessee (William Jennings Bryan) and the other defending the right of the teacher to teach scientific theories (Clarence Darrow).

Bryan, representing the creationist perspective, was arguing from the position that the age of the earth was ascertainable through an analysis of the data provided in the Scripture. He argued that because the Bible is the Word of God and is infallible, any theory that attempted to describe the universe in any other terms is blasphemous and deceitful. The argument was set up as "if you are against my position, you are against God, and if you are against God, you are obviously wrong." How often we notice that church leaders use that same form of reasoning to draw lines of exclusion by attributing divine approval to their interpretation of belief, and placing all others outside the fence of those who are righteous.

One particular argument that came from the defense attorney, Clarence Darrow, provided a reframing of the argument that has proved helpful to me as I work within the context of science and faith. Darrow argued from within the Scripture to address the age of the earth and to provide a context in which science and faith could interact. Consider this paraphrase of the argument from that movie. Darrow had Bryan on the stand for cross-examination. Clarence Darrow has been up all night reading his Bible in preparation for his line of questioning.

Darrow: Are you aware that scientists have discovered rocks that appear to be millions of years old?

Bryan: I, sir, am more interested in the "Rock of Ages" than I am in the age of rocks. *(laughter from the courtroom)*

Darrow: Since you are the expert here on the Scriptures, is it all right if I ask you a question about them?

Bryan: I would be more than happy to open the Holy Scriptures for you.

Darrow: Thank you, then I will proceed. The Bible tells us that the heavens and the earth were created in six days, plus that day of rest at the end.

Bryan: That is absolutely correct.

Darrow: Now, how long is a day?

Bryan: *(smugly)* Twenty-four hours.

Darrow: And what determines the length of a day? Isn't it the length of time that it takes for the earth to rotate on its axis in relation to the position of the sun?

Bryan: That is correct.

Darrow: Let me ask this, what day was it that the sun and the stars were created? Wasn't it on the third day?

Bryan: That is correct.

Darrow: Well, then, without the sun being in relation to the earth – that sort of changes things a little. I was wondering, is it possible that that day and those preceding days weren't exactly twenty-four hours each? Could it have possibly been twenty-five hours? I mean without a sun as a point of reference for day and night...

Bryan: *(slightly agitated)* Yes that is a possibility.

Darrow: Then is it also a possibility that that day could have been longer than that?

Bryan: I guess it is possible. I don't really see what bearing this line of reasoning has on the argument.

Darrow: If it is possible that the day was twenty-five hours, who is to say that it couldn't have been five billion years? After all, what is five billion years in the experience of an eternal God?

Darrow is effective because he doesn't challenge the scriptural perspective He adopts it, and he challenges William Jennings Bryan's position on his own terms. He begins from the position that Scripture is authoritative and that God created. Then he goes on to use rational inquiry to demonstrate that this particular perspective cannot, by Scripture, support its own claim. Yet this is not some kind of victory for the cause of reason against Scripture; rather, it is an argument that liberates the biblical perspective and opens the possibility of a new understanding, opening a large area for science and reason to work within the biblical perspective.

I often share this story with people who are attending the "Discovering Grace" class and inquiring about membership. The response to the issue is amazing. People look like they have light bulbs glowing in their eyes. "You mean it isn't blasphemous to see evolution in the context of creation and creation in the context of evolution?" It seems that they feel freed to give themselves more fully to God's story when they don't think that they are selling out their rational minds. An understanding of a creative God who brought everything into being must not be something that we can understand completely. If we could understand it completely, it wouldn't be faith. It would be knowledge. Creation doesn't need to pull us into this kind of contradiction that says either scientific truth or Christian truth. God is the creator of all truth … and that is the best *Perspective*.

How reason helps us tell the story

One of the most significant tensions between the church and the world is in the source of truth. There is an apparent contradiction between the truth claims of modernity and the truth expressed in the biblical story. Ever since the rise of modern science, and accelerating during the Age of Enlightenment, a conflict widens between Christianity and the claims of the modern world. This apparent conflict poses a particular challenge to a congregation that is ordered to "go into all the world and make disciples," to be relevant to a culture that does not speak our language. This is a time of high exposure to education and information. In many cases, thinking people are turned off by a church that is anti-intellectual, or a church that expects people to check their brains at the door. How can we as leaders make sure that reason is one of the sources of color from which we draw?

The writer of the Gospel of John was faced with the same dilemma. Greek culture was grounded in rational thought. The philosophers and the metaphysicians harbored thoughts about ultimate things. Platonic thought dominated the worldview of the Greek people. When they thought of creation, they thought in terms of *logos*, which was the original ordering principle of all things. They understood life to be created out of unformed stuff and pure reason, or *logos*. In the beginning, *logos* (pure reason, or *word*) spoke or touched the unformed stuff and created physical reality. They equated pure reason with light and the purely material with darkness.

In the context of an educated culture that esteemed reason, the Gospel writer took a different approach. He didn't alter the truth

of the story of God and Christ, but he reframed their understanding in a way that the biblical narrative set the stage. He used
reason to interpret faith for a particular culture. Look at this:

> In the beginning was the *Word* (logos), and the <u>Word was
> with God</u>, and the <u>Word was God</u> [*emphasis added*]. He was
> in the beginning with God. All things came into being
> through him, and without him not one thing came into
> being. What has come into being in him was life, and the
> life was the *light* of all people. The *light shines in the dark-*
> *ness, and the darkness did not overcome it.*
>
> There was a man sent from God, whose name was John.
> He came as a witness to testify to the light, so that all might
> believe through him. He himself was not the light, but he
> came to testify to the light. *The true light, which enlightens*
> *everyone, was coming into the world.*
>
> He was in the world, and the world came into being
> through him; yet the world did not know him. He came to
> what was his own, and his own people did not accept him.
> *But to all who received him, who believed in his name, he gave*
> *power to become children of God,* who were born, not of
> blood or of the will of the flesh or of the will of man, but of
> God.
>
> And the *Word became flesh and lived among us,* and we
> have seen his glory, the glory as of a father's only son, full
> of grace and truth. John 1:1-14

The writer of the Gospel of John used *reason* to enter the
Greek mind and make room for the truth of the Gospel. The
writer didn't say dump your story about the origins of the universe and replace it with mine. He didn't say, "If you died tonight,
do you know where you would go?" He didn't say, "You must get
into my aquarium or you are going to hell!" He said, "I understand the way you see life and reality. Let me help reframe it so
that you can see the larger context." The Gospel of John did not
inspire conflict with the Christian community that was forming
in the Hellenistic culture (though that conflict did emerge a cou-

ple hundred years later when Christians chose to fight among themselves over who had the most accurate knowledge). The Gospel of John is in conversation with reasonable people. This story of creation is not about making a decision or choosing who would rule over the others. John's gospel inspires a discussion. It isn't about leading the losers to the Lord. It is about adding leaven in their loaf.

Why is it important to rehash the tension between religion and science when explaining human and divine origins? Because the more things change, the more they stay the same. When I am preaching, leading worship, teaching a class, or even having a conversation at a restaurant or an airport, I am most likely talking with the equivalent of a postmodern Neo-Platonist. I am speaking with people who swim in the saltwater of education and reason but who also have a hunger for spirituality and mystery. We live with a certain comfort in the presence of mystery, but we can't ignore reason. Neither is it healthy to compartmentalize and say, "O.K. when I'm in the world, I can use my brain, but when I am at church I have to accept ideas blindly—even if they don't make sense." The task of the ImageSmith is to paint carefully with perspective, drawing from reason as one of the nuances of color that provides access for these people to the story of creation and redemption.

Reason and mystery

The modern era taught us to think that all the problems of humanity could be solved by the application of reason. We could understand nature through the various sciences. We could overcome disease, given the right tools and enough time and money for research. At times the church attempts to make room for reason by explaining away each of the miracles. Throughout the twentieth century, some scholars thought that if we could explain the miracles in terms of natural science, then we would be able to demonstrate that Christianity is valid, because the truth claims of religion are not contradictory to a modern worldview.

Reason and Scripture often have remained enemies, with church leaders forcing us to chose either faith or science. They are not mutually exclusive, however, for the context must be reframed, which allows them to exist as organically interrelated ways of understanding our environment.

When my son was three years old, he and I went on a camping trip. As we drove along, we were listening to a cassette tape about dinosaurs. There were songs about different types of dinosaurs, naming the dinosaurs, and famous paleontologists. The sun was shining. The tape was playing. We were singing along… *"Who named the dinosaurs? We know…"* It seemed like a great day to be alive. Then something happened that jolted me from my calm drive down the sunny side of the street. That little voice that I usually associated with toddler conversation spoke words that I was not, at that moment, prepared to hear.

In that sweet little-boy voice, he asked, "Dad, who's going to find our bones?"

I looked in the rearview mirror to make sure that he was indeed the one who had posed such a question. There he sat in the car seat with red around his mouth from the sucker he had just consumed, blond curls catching the sun, and bouncing as the car made its way along the road.

"What do you mean, son?" I responded (perhaps stalling for time).

"You know, like the *paleontologists* found the dinosaur's bones—who is going to find our bones?"

For some reason, I was not expecting this question from a child. His question took me abruptly from experiencing an easy drive on a beautiful day, with a child nearing his fourth year, to reflecting on the nature of time, the nature of change, and the relationship of scriptural eschatology (study of the end times) to natural science. It was his fault. From the back seat, from the mouth of my little boy, came words that set before me a dilemma. It is a dilemma that teases many in and around the church as they ponder whether or not this life is all there is, or if there is life after the grave.

Reason cannot tell us everything. Biblical stories capture the reality of the divine human relationship in a way that is beyond rational definition. The stories establish a perspective that is beyond reason.

Reason interprets the story

In this postmodern time, reason plays a different role. Reason helps us answer the questions: Does what we profess to believe make sense? Is there coherence in the beliefs that we hold? What are the applications to life? Who are we as God's people? Who are we as a church? Who are we as members of this particular religious tradition? Who are we as a congregation, and what difference does this make in the way we shape our ministry and live in the world? What does it mean to be saved? Saved from what? What does it mean to live in a grace-filled world? The role of reason is not to be the keeper of right doctrine, but the organizer of the story, the grid work of perspective. Visual leaders help people think theologically in ways that make a difference to their perception of reality and their daily decision-making. In all these cases, reason works within a faith perspective. Reason functions within the context of God's story.

On not checking your brain at the door

After a worship service, a visitor came up to speak with me. He had a background in science and astronomy. He said, "I've been in and out of churches through much of my life. It seemed like wherever I went, if I wanted to hold on to the stuff that made sense, the stuff that I've learned about in school, and the stuff that I've witnessed in the lab, then I had to nearly reject the truth of what the church was teaching. Or if the church was teaching something, and I wanted to be part of that church, then I had to nearly reject the truth that I knew made sense. But when I walked in here one day and you said, 'God doesn't expect you to check your brain at the door...' now that was an off-handed kind of comment. '*God doesn't expect you to check your brain at the door*.' But this is the first time I have heard that said in church."

God has given each of us a brain to use and a life that cries out to be understood. Not so that we will not be fooled and not believe in faith but so that we can live in the abundance and full-ness of this life. Religious truth need not stand over and against scientific truth. Educated, thinking people feel this struggle when they approach the church. Thus the visual leader incorpo-rates reason into his or her communication, and the ImageSmith provides access to the sacred story for those who swim in the postmodern sea of knowledge without significance.

It is refreshing for an ImageSmith to hear an intelligent person say, "Now I can draw close to the stories of God, which guide and ground my life, without having to jettison the stuff that is real, that I've learned."

This organic co-existence of science and faith is a beautiful birth of Jesus into the world, even here and now. The birth of Jesus initiated a tension between the old and the new in more ways than one. The canvas, our environment, is a crucible of shades, pigments, and techniques that, taken together, provide real depth and richness for the people that we lead.

Rent *Inherit the Wind* and watch the courtroom drama between Spencer Tracy and Fredric March. What are the arguments? What do you believe?

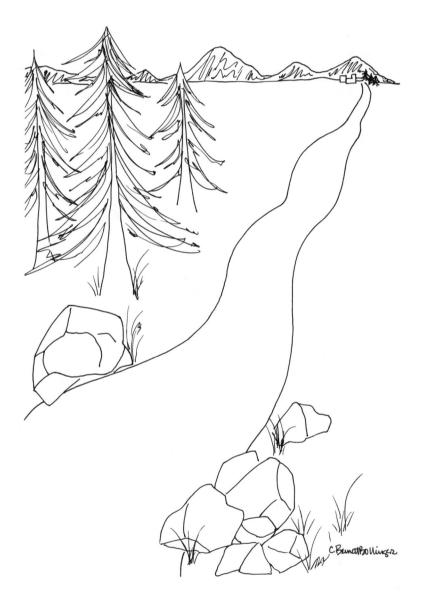

CHAPTER SEVEN

Entering the Artwork: Experience

With the sky painted, the horizon silhouetted, and the perspective in place, next my grandfather would begin to paint the foreground. The foreground is usually what draws a person to focus on the picture. There are several ways you can relate to a piece of art. You can judge it: "I like it or I don't like it." It strikes you as aesthetically pleasing or not. You can compare it to other works of art to see what genre or form it takes and what the influences on the artist might be. You can try to imagine what the artist imagined and was communicating when he or she created the work. Or you can enter the world of the art and look around. Art invites participation and experience at a variety of levels. Likewise, there are many ways that a person can enter into the experience of God's story. The ImageSmith must be aware that there is a diversity in spiritual experiences, and help provide people with access to the story on a variety of levels.

Experience and understanding

My mother enjoys retelling the story about a time when I was very little, perhaps three or four, and she was teaching me about traffic safety. She was about to wash clothes and wanted to be sure that I wouldn't go wandering off and get into danger. She took me by the hand and showed me the street. When a car came by she said, "Did you see that big car?"

"Mmm Hmm," I replied, nodding my head.

"If you go out in the street, you'll get run over, and we wouldn't want that, would we?"

"Mmm Mmm," I said, moving my head from side to side.

"While I'm washing clothes, don't you go out in the street, O.K.?"

"O.K., Mommy."

Off she went to wash the clothes. After a little while, I came into the laundry room, having driven my trike in the street, and told her proudly, "I din't get wunned over."

Part of the nature of being human is that we want to experience something for ourselves before we can truly believe it, before we can truly understand. No matter how carefully it is explained, it is hard to understand love if you haven't experienced it. No matter how well described, it is hard to know what green is if you haven't seen it. No matter how many pictures you have seen, it is impossible to grasp the awesome presence of the Grand Canyon until you have been there. And it is impossible to fully embrace the reality of the grace of God unless you experience it.

With experience as one of the nuances of color for the ImageSmith, we examine two different dimensions: the witness of the Spirit and the hospitality of spiritual gifts.

Witness of the Spirit

Because of the strong focus on knowledge and intellect, many of our religious activities have taken on an academic structure. Sunday School classes and even worship services tend towards the *listen and read* model. This is not a bad model for some things, but there is a large part of being human that is missed when all we can do is sit still and listen, responding as directed in the bulletin, reading what someone else has written and standing when designated by the * in the margin. When I speak with persons who are coming to church for the first time in their lives or returning after a long absence, they tell me they want to *experience God* in their lives and *grow spiritually*. People feel something missing and hope that they can find it in the church. The ImageSmith understands this hunger for spiritual experience, and establishes an environment that nurtures such experiences.

Experience was an important dimension of faith for John Wesley. Two particular experiences stood out in his early life as formative. Having been reared in the church, and trained for the ministry, Wesley understood well the practices and doctrines of Christianity. He was disciplined in prayer, study, and service. However, he came face to face with his lack of certainty while on the boat between Bristol and Savannah. During the voyage, a huge storm threatened to sink the ship. Wesley and most of the other passengers were terrified by the power of the storm and the threat of death at sea. During the storm, he saw a group of Moravian Christians in prayer, seemingly fearless in the face of danger and death. He wondered what it was in their faith that allowed them to be so calm and to have such peace rather than the terrible fear he felt. He was missing out on something. When he discussed the event with the Moravian pastor, Wesley learned of the witness of the Spirit and the inner assurance of faith. These things were foreign to him.

Upon returning to England from Savannah, Wesley had an experience of personal and relational salvation that opened his eyes to a life with God that was based on more than an intellectual understanding of theology and on following the rules of the church and the commandments of the Scripture. It was also based on a *personal experience of saving faith.* The experience happened during a small group meeting in a house on Aldersgate Street during the reading of Martin Luther's preface to the letter to the Romans, which focused on salvation by faith rather than salvation by works. This was an important, mysterious, and warm experience; but did not lead him to reject his earlier dedication to the traditions, practices, and rules of the church. The assurance came in a setting that comforted him as a pious scholar, while someone was reading a biblical commentary to the group. He realized that hope is based in faith and not in works. He did not stray, however, from his strict practices of piety, to which he had so long been committed since Oxford. This experience provided a new dimension to his faith and the missing link in his relationship with God, which could not be connected merely through rigorous methods.

The hospitality of spiritual experiences

During my first year in college, I went to a Trappist Monastery in Conyers, Georgia. I was 18. I had a professor who took the time to listen to my spiritual questions and introduced me to Thomas Merton. Then he told me of a monastery that was just a few miles from the college and that they had a place for visitors and guests to stay. I made a little sign that said monastery and hitchhiked there. The man who had stopped to pick me up drove down the long entryway lined with magnolias and dropped me off at the guesthouse.

"Hello," I said to the robed Trappist behind the counter (not knowing whether or not he would speak because of the vow of silence they take).

He did speak. "Welcome."

"I heard you had rooms for guests."

"That's right. Will you be staying with us?"

"Yes, please, if that is all right."

"Oh, yes, you are welcome here."

He didn't ask for a driver's license. He didn't inquire how I would be paying for my stay. He didn't ask how many nights I would be staying. He simply welcomed me. He then showed me the dining room, told me of mealtimes, pointed out the library and the room with tapes of various speakers. He told me where the chapel was and that I was welcome to join in any of the worship services. I followed him upstairs and then down the hall where he pointed out the showers, the restroom, and my room.

He left me alone.

I was in a small room with a bed, a sink, a little dresser and a nightstand with a lamp. On the wall hung a crucifix. As a Protestant, I was not used to the version with the dead Messiah hanging there. Somehow that added a feeling of uneasiness and despair to the otherwise warm and hospitable moment.

I sat down on the bed. What now? It was quiet. There was no one else on the entire floor. No stereo. No radio. No TV. No roommate. No homework. No transportation.

An unfamiliar sound drifted into my awareness and stirred my attention. It sounded like Gregorian chants echoing through the screened window and through the hall. I couldn't tell the direction of the sound. It seemed to be surrounding me. I lay there still, listening for a long time. The room gradually began to darken as the sun set. A beam of orange sun pierced the Venetian blinds, striping the wall with light and causing the crucifix to cast a long shadow. It was a bit eerie. Chanting coming from I knew not where; crucifix with lifeless, pained, and broken body and crown of thorns; angled stripes of light and pronounced shadows. All alone in a strange place.

The chanting suddenly stopped. Then my whole body clenched as I heard a woman scream...Aaahhhhhhh! A blood-curdling scream. And again... Aaahhhhhh! Chanting, crucifixes, screaming... My heart began to pound, my mind to race, and I began to imagine what was happening. Eerie lighting... men in robes... chanting... a woman screaming. Oh my God! What have I gotten myself into? My senses were peaked. There was more chanting and the screaming stopped. I sat there listening until I finally fell asleep.

I came to consciousness the next morning while it was still dark. I got out of bed and went outside for a walk. The sky was pinkish across the horizon. The sun was not quite up yet, but morning was coming. The moon was still visible and a light mist was rising from the lake. I walked in silence, reflecting on the experience from the night before, and I wondered, "What was it that I heard? What was going on, and whom can I call to come get me out of this place?" I took a deep breath and started to pray silently, allowing the still beauty of the morning to flood my being and bring stillness and a peace to my agitated soul.

The first ray of light crested the horizon and shot arrow-like through the tall pines under which I stood. Then, directly behind me and much louder than the night before, I heard the same, piercing, blood-curdling scream. I whirled around to face the horror and came face to face with...a peacock. It was a peacock who said goodnight to the sun when the orange rays peeked over the horizon and good morning when the first rays of the new day appeared. That was his pattern of morning and evening praise. Though I was still a little freaked out, I decided to stay, and am glad I did.

What I found there was a space designed with a spiritual hospitality that invited me into God's story on a variety of levels. I could choose which one spoke to me at the moment. Some were planned. Some were purely serendipitous. It was a spirituality playground with all types of doorways into God's story. Gardens, bonsai trees in the greenhouse, beautiful grounds, places of silence and solitude, good reading material, and comfortable places to sit and read. The architecture evoked peace and pointed to the Holy. There was a pattern of five worship services spread throughout the day.

I found portals of entry into God's story for every dimension of being. There were opportunities to enter into the story intellectually through reading or listening to lectures on tape. They demonstrated ways to enter through devotional practice and stillness. All around were ways to enter through the beauty of creation, by walking in the woods or on the grounds, or by gardening or tending a bonsai. Opportunities for shared meals and spiritual conversation provided relational entry into God's story. Artwork and statuary provided opportunities for reflection and meditation. Around the walls of the chapel were the "*stations of the cross.*" There was the worship, which varied in focus and flow, including music, scripture, liturgy, silence, and word. The place had been designed for *spiritual hospitality*. Practically every sense was invited and welcomed to enter the story of God.

These were powerful experiences, but they don't happen only at the monastery. As we teach, lead, and design experiences, we can make room for mystery and create portals of spiritual hospitality for different spiritual types.[1] Different people are drawn into God's story through a variety of different practices and experiences such as:

- Prayer
- Guided meditation
- *Lectio divina* (entering the Scripture)
- Shared meals
- Spiritual conversation
- Silence
- Meditation

- Making crosses
- Preparing emergency items for disaster response
- Baking bread for visitors or the homebound
- Reflection
- Going on retreat
- Walking the labyrinth
- Painting
- Planting
- Gardening
- Designing altars
- Singing
- Journaling
- Writing prayers
- Taking pictures for worship or teaching

The one-size-fits-all approach to spiritual experiences and corporate worship design does not work any longer. Human and cultural experience is so diverse that visual leaders must offer a variety of entry points into the story.

Hospitality at Hope

The presentational modes of worship popularized by Willow Creek's early "seeker services" are not as attractive to the younger crowd. Whereas unchurched Boomers were content to attend worship in an anonymous setting and sit and watch an entertaining presentation and receive information about God and Jesus, the younger generations long for something more "real." They say that they have had enough virtual reality and that they are tired of neatly packaged product presentations of life. What they are looking for is honesty and reality and story. They want to be around real people and join them in experiencing community, forgiveness, caring, worship and God's presence. There is a hunger for experience of the Holy. Things become true when they are experienced.

Hope Presbyterian Church in Cordova, Tennessee, was started in 1992 and currently has over 5,000 in attendance each weekend. The original worship service is presented in a Boomer style: casual dress, informal language, humor, praise music and a practical, applied Bible message. Recently, they have started a newer service for the twenty-somethings. The format for the new service is very different. The chairs are removed from the worship area. Oriental rugs are brought in. People gather in small groups on the rugs around candles. There is a mixture of musical styles, including Taizé singing and acoustic guitar. Digital imagery is sometimes projected on large screens to add another dimension to the experience. There are times of congregational prayer and silence. The pastor shares an interactive message and helps facilitate discussion. This is one example of a church that is trying to create a multisensory, interactive experience to address the hunger for spiritual relevance.

Not all churches need to chuck the pews and buy a truckload of rugs and candles. This approach wouldn't work everywhere, and these twenty-somethings might prefer to park themselves in comfortable chairs when they reach their forties, but it raises the important question that often gets lost when we find a formula that works: How do we as leaders add the dimension of experience to the matrix of our congregational culture? How can we offer the hospitality of spiritual experience through our communication, our worship, our facilities and our opportunities for involvement?

Placing spiritual hyperlinks on everyday life

Several members of the congregation were at work turning the woods in front of the church into a prayer garden. One day I invited people to help by hauling compost, which is not a glamorous task. And it is hard to motivate people to get up at 7 A.M. on Saturday morning to go down and pick up free compost from the recycling center. Instead of apologizing or begging, I decided to paint a picture of hauling compost, which is connected with the rhythms of the earth and the unfolding of God's work in the world.

You can either see it as merely hauling the compost—putting it in a truck, driving it there, and dumping it in a hole—or you can enter the picture and look at it with different eyes. You might see it as an act of spiritual servanthood. You would be helping to create a place of beauty where children could walk with their grandparents, people could go to pray, or those who are broken or hurting might find a place to experience closeness to God, the movement of the seasons, and the beauty of creation. People may experience the power and the presence of God because of hauling compost.

I placed a spiritual hyperlink on a mundane task, and people clicked. A simple task was transformed by the experience of walking in that garden, the rhythms of creation, and the way God has provided beauty for us.

I did not ask anyone to believe a particular set of creeds, or to do something that was their duty, or make them feel guilty if they didn't do it. It was an experience that could be grasped by a biblically illiterate person, a deeply versed nature lover, a seeker, or by someone broken and hurting. It had handles for many people to see and to touch, to feel and experience; handles not only in the past but in ways in which they could be involved in a simple activity, a bite-size piece of interplay with the processes of creation and God's interaction with humanity. I painted the foreground of life so that the workers would have the opportunity to experience God's story.

Maintaining balance

Overemphasizing experience can create imbalance in four ways: 1) we might create experience junkies, 2) we might make particular experiences normative as a test for spiritual authenticity, 3) we might depress or ignore intellectual engagement, and 4) we might avoid the continuity of liturgical and sacramental practice in worship.

Experience Junkies

An experience junkie is someone who has tasted a particular spiritual experience and spends the rest of his or her time trying to find another spiritual "high." I knew one very talented and wonderfully friendly young woman who was a spiritual junkie. She would appear to be living life smoothly, but then she'd find her way to some big revival meeting or a crusade and get saved. It was always a highly emotional experience. She would return to church, get very involved, then start to slip away. People would reach out to her and try to help her stay connected, but she would fall away. Before long, though, she would return from another revival or crusade or retreat or something that gave her a spiritual high. Her spiritual life was out of balance. She became addicted to the experience of "being saved." Missing was the dimension of growth in her life of faith. She needed connection with the community and the patterns of development: habits of religious life, sacraments, personal disciplines, an increasing understanding of what it means to be a Christian, and how to interpret life theologically.

Some congregations encourage this kind of addiction to experience by establishing a pattern of worship that constantly recalls "backsliding" Christians.

Making particular experiences normative

Once I was visiting with a woman who had not been involved in a church for a very long time. She had not been able to bring herself to participate in the life of any church because of some negative experiences she had as a child. She was raised by her grandmother in a small, independent, Pentecostal church. Church membership was based on receiving baptism by the Holy Spirit, marked by speaking in tongues. As she grew up, she said she always felt uncomfortable in the church, and somewhat frightened.

They didn't have a scheduled "confirmation," but they did have a service for young people who had not received the Spirit by a particular age. This special service of prayer and praise was designed to ask God to touch the youth who were not yet members. My friend was one of those for whom the service was designed. As Sunday drew closer, she became more and more worried about what was going to happen. What if she became frightened? What if nothing happened? Would she be rejected? Would she be ridiculed?

When the day came, her grandmother came to get her before the service. Finally, she got up the nerve to tell her grandmother of her concern: "What if nothing happens? What if I don't speak in tongues?" To this question her grandmother replied, "Oh, don't fret about it...just mumble somethin'; no one will ever know the difference."

The woman was crushed. She hadn't been able to trust the truth of Christianity for many years. In that church, the experience of speaking in tongues had been made normative to the point that it was more important to appear falsely to have received the *"gift"* than to be true to your own experience. God grants a variety of gifts and touches us in many different ways. No single experience is better than the other.

Beyond monochrome: intellectual depression

ImageSmiths will help churches in the postmodern era transcend attitudes of narrowness and compartmentalization and create an atmosphere of acceptance and the permission to think and question, doubt and disagree. One tendency of the modern perspective was to view things as true or false, right or wrong. Postmodernism has taught us about the validity of multiple perspectives, which is of course an ancient idea. I find it refreshing that the monastery welcomed me, housed me, fed me, and opened for me the doors of spiritual hospitality but never once asked if I was a Catholic, a Christian, or what I believed.

I am amazed at the theological diversity in the congregation I serve. There are persons who have come from the Unitarian church and others from a Pentecostal background. There is richness and a blessing that comes from making room for diverse perspectives. There is also some inevitable tension, but we try to emphasize the value of openness, acceptance, discussion, and learning from one another. Another dimension of spiritual hospitality is hospitality toward the stranger's perspective.

As Wesley struggled with the issue of diversity within the Christian community and the relationship between Christians and non-Christians, he touched on an issue that relates directly to our current situation. In his sermon on the Catholic Spirit, he

discusses the difficulties of practicing the scriptural commandment to "love one another":

> 3. All men approve of this; but do all men practise it?
> Daily experience shows the contrary. Where are even the
> Christians who "love one another as He hath given us
> commandment?" How many hinderances lie in the way!
> The two grand, general hinderances are, First, that they
> cannot all think alike; and, in consequence of this,
> Secondly, they cannot all walk alike; but in several
> smaller points their practice must differ in proportion to
> the difference of their sentiments.
> 4. But although a difference in opinions or modes of
> worship may prevent an entire external union; yet need
> it prevent our union in affection? Though we cannot
> think alike, may we not love alike? May we not be of one
> heart, though we are not of one opinion? Without all
> doubt, we may. Herein all the children of God may unite,
> notwithstanding these smaller differences. These
> remaining as they are, they may forward one another in
> love and in good works.[2]

These words address the need for an attitude of mutual
acceptance in the midst of our diversity, as we work to maintain
grounding in the story that is our common treasure. It is another
point of creative tension, another place of process and interplay,
another place where we enter the creative dance of faith.

The continuity of spiritual and liturgical practice

As leader it is important to remember that while people get
excited about new experiences, they are still creatures of habit.
There is something important about ritual, pattern, and order. A
patterned spiritual life can provide access to the artwork of God's
presence in powerful ways. The order of prayer, song, and silence
at the monastery was an oasis of refreshment for my soul.
Sacraments, patterned prayer, and the rhythm of worship provide

regular access to the sustaining experience of God's presence. The patterns and disciplines are important because they create opportunities to "enter the artwork" that are not based on high energy worship services, recurring journeys down the "sawdust trail" (tent revival), or other heightened, infrequent experiences.

Patterned spirituality and liturgical continuity do not necessarily mean strict adherence to one particular form of worship or liturgy, but familiar elements present in worship and in life are necessary. I have preached on several occasions at the retirement community chapel near our church. Many of the residents are active and conversant; however, many who attend the services depend on someone to roll them down in their wheel chairs. Some of them sit with unbroken gaze, starring off into some other place. Sometimes their state makes me question whether or not they are aware of what is happening at the service at all. Yet, when a familiar hymn is sung, or the Lord's Prayer is spoken, most of them at least brighten, and many times join in. Familiar patterns of spirituality and liturgy provide a richness of experience that transcends our immediate awareness. It is important that leaders help people see and develop a pattern of sustainable access to the ongoing touch of God.

The story of God's activity is rich and complex, yet it is beautiful in its complexity. Through the model of the artist who paints the sky first, silhouettes the horizon, paints with perspective, and invites entry into the artwork, we see a model for pointing to a larger picture of our setting in the activity of God. The ImageSmith helps people see the setting of the Scripture, the silhouettes of tradition, the perspective of reason, and helps people find their way into the foreground of God's story.

Notes

[1]Kent Ira Groff has a great resource, *The Soul of Tomorrow's Church* (Nashville: Upper Room Books, 2000), for developing different spiritual practices and experiences for use in a variety of ministry settings. Also, The *Companions in Christ* Series (Nashville, Upper Room) is an excellent small-group resource to explore the classic spiritual disciplines together.

[2]Edward H. Sugden, ed., *John Wesley's Fifty-three Sermons* (Nashville: Abingdon Press, 1983), 493.

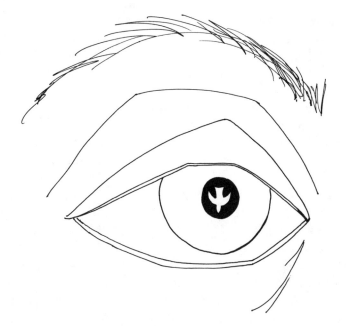

C.BennettBollinger

CHAPTER EIGHT

Seeing into Being

While playing one of those high-speed racing video games with my son, I soon realized that if I focused on the immediacy of the other cars moving at 200 hundred miles an hour right around me, I was bound to swerve and wreck, or drive in a reactive way and end up losing the game. I discovered that I needed to keep focused on the emerging horizon so that I would have time to *anticipate and prepare for change* instead of simply reacting. The same seems to be true in leadership. Unless I focus on the horizon and keep a sense of perspective about the changes in the future, my leadership will be frenetic and reactive, as opposed to purposeful, smooth, guided, and able to draw people into the mission. Effectiveness depends on where I focus—how I orient my vision.

Seeing the vision

God gives vision. It doesn't come from a desire to do something good, or something worthwhile. Vision is a gift of the Creator who calls us into the life of sharing the task of creation. Though leaders in business, the sciences, or the arts might act as if their passion and commitments are self-induced, vision is also a gift from God for the everyday ministries of the laity, as ordinary people go about their work in God's creation. Leaders in and beyond the church must be open and available to God through listening, prayer, and keeping watch for vision and direction. Sometimes it comes slowly. Sometimes it is clear and immediate. Sometimes it is given to one person, and sometimes it comes from the discernment of a community. Vision comes in different ways, but when it is of God, it carries a certain energy and urgency that commands attention. God showed Ezekiel a vision. It was a strange and complex vision (Ezekiel 1). It was a vision that might have frightened many people. It certainly would have seemed to the one receiving the vision and the one with whom the information was being shared to be on the bizarre side of expression. It was a vision of a chariot made with creatures and crystal wheels above which floated the presence of the Lord. God gave Ezekiel some specific directions about what he was supposed to do. This vision showed Ezekiel that he was about to do something that he would not do on his own. It was something in which God would be present, and would guide and bless—if Ezekiel remained faithful to what God was showing him. Required is an openness to God, an unwavering faithfulness to God's direction, and a willingness to speak it to God's people without reservation.

Moses also received a vision from God that became his calling. Remember Moses and his encounter with the burning bush? No one else saw that sight. Moses alone had the chat with the divine bush-flambeaux, yet the strength and source of his leadership came from the divine encounter. He led with the living memory of the burning bush. Sometimes the divine encounter sustains us for leadership; sometimes it becomes a vision for the future.

Painting the future by pointing to possibility

In 1992 I was appointed to start a new church. There were no members with which to start other than my wife, and one friend who was moving to the area to go to college. It is a strange feeling to be sent to something that doesn't exist. In some way, I understand a little better what Abram must have felt when God said, "Go to a land I will show you." (Genesis 12:1 NIV). I wasn't exactly sure what to do, but to pray, to listen, to watch, and to follow what I heard. There were times when I didn't know what to do next.

As we started to form what would be the core of the congregation, we needed some way of sharing information. I began meeting with people and sharing ideas and dreams, as well as asking people to assemble friends for evenings of visioning and sharing. As a core of interested people emerged, it became necessary to develop a way of communicating with them on a regular basis. Because there were no regular meetings to which everyone came, I decided to begin a newsletter. I had produced newsletters before, and that seemed an effective tool for communication in this setting.

The strange thing about writing a newsletter for a church that doesn't exist, however, is an awkward limitation to available material. There were opportunities for people to share resources and musical abilities. There were announcements about upcoming meetings and things like that, but there was not much else on our calendar. Even though there weren't many events or activities or other things to coordinate and schedule, it was important to communicate as a group with those who were expressing interest. I thought about the needs of the congregation, or rather of those who would make up the congregation (when we actually got around to having one), and decided that we needed a *picture of the future.* We needed something to hold in our minds and hearts. It should be motivating but not too specific, so as not to lock us into one particular outcome. We needed a glimpse into the future.

I went out to the land chosen for the future church building. The front corner of the land had once been a trailer park. The rest of it was tall pines and vines and all of the other underbrush that accompanies unimproved forest in Louisiana. I stood where a trailer once had been and looked off into the woods. What would be there? What was God trying to do in this place and in this time? I prayed and asked God to be with us. I prayed for those who might be touched by the community of faith that God was trying to create here. Then I listened with ears, eyes, and heart toward the future. As I stood there, I could begin to imag-

ine, or see an image of a church. There among the trees, I saw it.
I couldn't describe it physically, but I began to see the dream take
shape. Back at the office, seated at the computer, I began to paint
the future with words—words that would begin to build potential in the collective mind of the ones God was calling to this new
adventure. When those on the mailing list received their first
newsletter, they read these words:

YOU CAN BE PART OF SOMETHING GREAT!

There is nothing more exciting, rewarding, fulfilling or
meaningful that we could be involved in right now than
being involved in the starting of a NEW CHURCH. Just
think about it… to be part of the creation of something that
will provide a place for people, young and old, to gather,
learn, fellowship, worship, serve, celebrate, laugh, cry, love
and grow in God. Imagine being part of the creation of
something that will influence generations of people in and
beyond this community. It is truly an exciting time to be a
part of the things that are happening in South Shreveport.

Sometimes I go out to the church property and stand
there and try to let God look at the property through my
eyes and let me know what is supposed to be there. As I
stand there amidst the spreading oaks and the towering
pines, listening to the birds and feeling the soft breeze, it is
easy for me to hear the laughter of children playing on the
playground that will be built, and to hear the joyful music
of worship and celebration coming out of the full sanctuary
that has yet to be designed. There is so much to be seen and
so much to be done… As we dream together about what
kind of church we are creating, we need to keep foremost
in our minds the words that Solomon wrote in Psalm 127:
"*Unless the Lord builds the house, they who build it labor in
vain.*" It is easy to get caught up in thinking about what "I"
would like this church to do and be, and dreaming and
thinking about the buildings, and so forth, that we put the
cart before the horse. The most important thing to remem-

ber as we go about the task of building this church is that while it is our church... it is first of all God's church. I hope our prayer will be: "God, give me eyes to see your vision, a heart to know your will, and the courage and selflessness that would enable me to live first and foremost for you. Lord, use me in ways you see fit, so that this church would become what you would have it to be."

New Directions Newsletter, Volume 1, Number 1, August 12, 1992

The newsletter, which every church staff produces, is an important dimension of painting a picture *of the future* in the minds of the congregation. People told me that after reading the article, they too would go over to the land and look, dream, and pray. They were beginning to look toward the future that had been there all along, waiting for God to draw our attention to it.

The canvas grows

A couple of months later, God gave another opportunity that enabled us to be more than we could have been if just dependent upon our own actions. I was working with a group of youth in a hunger relief team gleaning turnip greens (picking what is left over) to take to a soup kitchen. As we were working, a newspaper reporter came to do a story. We were all covered with sweat and dust from our work in the fields. She began to ask questions about why we were out in a field in the middle of summer instead of out doing something more "fun," like most of the people our age. (At the time I was wearing a bandana and some little round sunglasses so she thought I was one of the youth.) We told her that it was in response to the scripture in Deuteronomy:

> When you are harvesting in your field and you overlook a sheaf, do not go back to get it. Leave it for the alien, the fatherless and the widow, so that the LORD your God may bless you in all the work of your hands.
>
> Deuteronomy 24:19 NIV

She seemed a little surprised at the response and asked me, "How do you know so much about the Bible?"

"I'm a pastor."

"You're a pastor?!?!?!" She seemed surprised.

"Yes, I'm a pastor." I smiled at her expression, "This is just my 'youth gear.' You ought to do a story on the church I'm starting."

"You're starting a church?" Same look.

I told her about the plans for the church and my hope that it would draw many people who were not otherwise involved in church. She took my phone number and told me that she would get back with me.

About a week later, she called and told me she had spoken with the bishop and district superintendent and she wanted to come and interview me. "Wow!" I thought "She's serious." We arranged a time and met. She asked several questions and even sent a photographer to get a picture. It's a puzzling moment when the newspaper is doing a story on your church, but you don't really have one yet. Of what will they take a picture?

She thanked me for the interview, and she told me that the story would be in the paper on Monday. I was excited. An article in the paper, how great! Free publicity was much needed because we had only three thousand dollars as start-up money. I thought about what she might write. I prayed for the people who would read the article. I thanked God for the opportunity. I waited. I got anxious and impatient. By the time Sunday night rolled around I was too excited to sleep much at all. I managed to stay in bed until about 4:30 a.m. and then drove down to the corner store to get a paper.

"Morning."

"Morning."

"I'd like a copy of *The Times*, please."

"That'll be fifty cents."

"Here you are. Thank you." I handed the clerk the coins as calmly as I could, trying not to betray my desire to rip into the paper right then and there.

Once in the car I was free to open the paper and begin my search. I looked through the front section... then the local... then the sports... and, finally, through the features section....

Nothing. I found nothing. "Oh well," I thought, "maybe she meant next Monday." I folded the paper, tossed it on the passenger seat, and shifted into reverse. As I turned to look behind me, my eye caught something that I had not seen before. Right there on the front page—right beside "Saddam Hussein caves in to U.N. pressure" and "Olympic Gold Rush"—was a picture of a young pastor in a suit standing next to a tree—and a headline that read, "O, Come all Ye Faithful, Methodists start new church in new way." I couldn't believe it. There it was, right there on the front page (below the fold, but still…). The article spelled out the dreams I had shared with the reporter. There were positive words from others she had interviewed. On the inside, there was a map showing the exact location where the church *would* be and even a phone number to my answering machine.

I was stunned. I was amazed. I had been given an opportunity to paint into the minds of the entire community a picture of the possibilities of a church that didn't yet exist.

I haven't forgotten that morning. I never will. I retell the story every time I have a new member class. I share it and then ask the question, "Now, do things like that just happen, or does that seem like something more than that to you?" The responses are always similar "Wow, God really blessed you with that opportunity." "Front page coverage for a nonexistent church… that must have been God because that kind of thing doesn't happen by accident."

"That's right," I'll continue, "And if it is true that God had a plan for the beginnings of this congregation, then don't you think God is still active here? And, just as God called all of the folks who were the founders of the church, *perhaps God has drawn you here* for a purpose."

That story is a piece of the story that becomes a "shared memory" for the entire congregation. All are, through the retelling of the story, connected to the beginning. The sharing of memory and the sharing of story form a unifying bond for the members of our church, no matter when they come to be a part of what God is doing. Story has a power to help paint a new reality. It has the power to connect those in the present to a powerful past.

Building bridges to the future

Transitions are among the most important times in the life of the church, and one of the most important times for a leader to negotiate. The visual leadership of transitions makes use of the Scripture, connects us with history, and moves the community into the future, by using image, varied media, stories, and experience. The goal is to create a multi-layered experience that creates a shared sense of memory and identity.

Bridge through troubled waters

As we moved through the difficult time of designing, funding, and constructing our first facility, tension began to take its toll on the newly gathered group. It was important for us to build big enough to continue to grow, yet "big enough" equated in the minds of many as "too much money." Borrowing almost $1.5 million for the construction of a dream by a group of people who had been in existence only two years seemed like a risky idea to all of the bankers in town, and to many of the members of the congregation. After much searching, we located funding from a bank in a neighboring town, and decided, with great faith, to move forward with the plans. We had faith, yes, as well as great trepidation.

As the construction process progressed, the weather slowed us down, turning the construction site into a sea of impassable mud for a couple of months. I drove by the site every day. I would stare at that Martian-looking clay and the mud with a bulldozer sunk into it at an angle, looking like a drowning monster that is coming up for air. Construction delays and surprises made the process slower, more expensive, and more difficult. Finally, the ground dried enough for the foundation to be poured, but the difficulties continued. The stress was causing anxiety, and the anxiety began to erode the fabric of hope and vision that had enabled us to move so far so fast.

Church leaders were scheduled to meet to discuss our directions and to address our difficulties. I sensed that we were at a point of terribly important transition. If, as we gathered, we could recall the hope and vision that had guided us to this point, and grab hold of the grace of God who was beckoning us onward, then we would make it past this difficult time. If, however, people left the meeting, feeling negation, fear, and division, the path ahead would be very difficult. I knew we could make it. God was allowing me to see what was going on and what could be done. How could I help them see it as well?

In the gathering we talked about what it was that we were worried about, the amount of money that it was going to cost to build a building, the difficulties that we were having. I decided to tell people not just to see the immediate difficulties and the conflicts at hand but instead to experience a shared future into which they could move. We then made a trip over to the land. I asked everyone to walk out onto the foundation. I asked them to lie down on the concrete. Strangely, they obliged me. What a strange sight it must have been for anyone driving nearby: a group of adults who were lying around the cement foundation on a construction site. As they lay there, my task was painting the picture of the future so that they could walk into that future and have a shared experience of hope, vision, and success. I chose to use a guided meditation as a way to engage the group in the experience of a common scene.

Guided meditation: visioning for the new facility

"Don't be afraid," the prophet answered. "Those who are with us are more than those who are with them."

And Elisha prayed, "O LORD, open his eyes so he may see." Then the LORD opened the servant's eyes, and he looked and saw the hills full of horses and chariots of fire all around Elisha (2 Kings 6:16-17, NIV).

Close your eyes. Take a few deep breaths. Relax. Imagine yourself in your car. It is one year from today. You just finished a quick breakfast and you are on your way to church.

You smile as you think back to the days when you had to drive to Captain Shreve for church, never knowing what would be missing, or how the temperature in the building would be. It is so nice to be in our new facility.

You look at the building there amidst the trees. The turn signal clicks as your tires crunch across the rocks in the parking lot. So much has changed from the old days before the building...the spirit and the feeling are still the same, but having our own place has really set us free to expand and improve our ministries. If there is someone with you in the car... drop them off at the front. How are they received? How are they greeted? Knowing that it is important to keep the spaces close to the door for visitors, those with babies, or people with special needs, you wave at the parking lot greeter as you drive to the back lot. Notice the flowers and the landscaping. Notice how the grounds look and how they are kept. Thank heaven for those people who do the grounds ministry.

You park your car, and walk with some other people and their children. You hear the laughter, feel the warmth of the sun, and hear the birds chirping in the oak above your head. The sun is from the east, so the front of the building is bright and striped with the shadows of the tall pines just opposite the entryway. As you walk into the large gathering area, what do you hear? What do you smell? How are you greeted? Take some time to see whom you meet and greet them. What are people talking about?

At the welcome center, you are greeted by a woman who only a few months before hadn't been involved in church at all. Now she and her three children have found a home. "What brought you to Grace?" you ask. Listen as she tells you her story. As you turn to go look at the bulletin board with the pictures of the latest mission trip and other mission activities, the greeter hands you a list of church-related activities. Begin to read down the page. What do you see? What is going on in your ministry area? Small groups. Musical practices. Seminars. Support groups for people in the church and community. Sunday school classes. Notice

the number of worship services, the way they are scheduled. Are there new groups meeting? You also see a notice
of search for a new staff position; what is the position?

"Where's Rob?" someone asks. The music for the first
worship service is about to start. You decide to take a quick
look in the youth and children's wing, so you take a right
out of the gathering area and walk through the windowed
hall that looks through the greenery into the worship area.
You look into the gathering area for the kindergarden
through second grade. They are singing. Who is leading
them? How many kids are there? Is it set up? Upstairs you
glance into each of the elementary rooms. What do you
see? You walk into the youth gathering area. What are the
sounds in your ears? What do you see? "Have you seen
Rob?" "He was here just a minute ago. He went that way,"
says one of the teenagers, as she points to the stairs.

So, down you go, past the kitchen. Mmm, smell the coffee brewing. You'd love to stop there and have a cup and
visit with that man you met at your small group just a couple of days ago, but you are on a mission. Through the hall
by the nurseries, you see the signup sheets. Popping your
head into each room, you wonder how they keep up with
all those little ones.

The music has started, and a glance into the worship area
reveals that Rob still isn't in there. Quickly, you head over
into the adult Sunday School area. As you go, you notice
the carpet and the tile. It looks really nice. I wonder who
was on the clean team this week? Passing through, you
notice the names of the classes on the doors. Some have
more than one name on them because they are used more
than one time on Sunday mornings. You poke your head
into the office area and look down the hall. Rob's office door
is open, but he's not there. Glancing down, you pick up a
copy of last week's newsletter. You scan it as you walk... the
financial statement... another good week...

Rounding the corner into the gathering area one more
time, you enter the worship area. People are still coming in

the doors. You look across the people standing there, some singing, some visiting, to see that Rob is at the front talking to the family that is being baptized together today. He points them toward the little waterfall and tells them that it's right there that the baptism will take place. Relieved that there is a preacher there for the service, you relax and move toward the rest of your family or some friends. They saved you a place. You look around at the musicians, and the plants, the faces of the people, the banners, and the fabric that hangs down from the joists on the ceiling. The last chords of "Lord, Prepare Me to Be a Sanctuary" slowly fade. The projection on the screen up front changes—it is a video image of a deer by a mountain stream in the woods. Then, the words appear over the image of the deer. The music swells... "As the deer longeth for the waters, so my soul longeth after you. You alone are my heart's desire, and I long to worship You."

Joyful peace comes over you. The person beside you is a visitor. She doesn't have a clue about what was required to start this church—all the work and planning, the sacrifice and struggle. But something will happen to her this morning through the music, or through the sermon, or the atmosphere, or the Sunday school lesson. She will hear the voice of God, and she will give her heart to Christ.

You think back to those early days. Was it worth it? [*Long pause for reflection and listening.*] The last strains of "As the Deer" fade. Take the hands of the people next to you. Bow your head. "Lord, thank you that you are with us this morning. We know that you have something for each of us. We know that you have drawn us here for a reason. I thank you that you work with us, that you work in us, that you work on us and that you work through us. Thank you for the privilege of being your disciple... in the name of Jesus."

The change in perspective was immediate. Together, we had peered into the future. We were seeing it into being. That glimpse gave us the energy and the shared memory needed to send us forward once again. After our time at the building site, we returned to the rented storefront office where we washed each other's feet and had an opportunity to fix the story with servanthood. We saw together. And after our shared experience, we were able to paint a picture of the steps that would be required to move into that future. It was not a descriptive set of instructions and a pep-talk; it was providing the group with an opportunity to walk into that future personally, so they could see it and have a shared, mutual sense of experience out of which they could operate.

Bridges of Identity and Purpose

During the process of organizing and growing our congregation, there were several crucial moments of transition into the future where God was calling us. Without intentional actions during this process, we still would have moved into the future, but that future might have looked very different. Leading across bridges of transition also helps establish in the group a sense of the central values and shared identity that are critical to healthy continued development. One such time of transition involved the move from the temporary worship space at a high school to our new facility. Some people began saying we would have a real church now, so we would do things differently, dress differently, not take coffee into the sanctuary, and so forth. My intent as leader—even with things as trivial as a spill on the church carpet —is to help people build a common experience, a shared consensus of experience about a future that was not yet in existence. They could then move with an understanding of where they were going, instead of bringing preconceived notions of who they might need to become.

On the last day in the temporary location, we gathered together as an entire congregation. Instead of ending one day at the old place and beginning the next time at the new place, we had a *service of transition*. Especially for times of transition, the Bible stories can become the framework for new experiences. On this occasion, we chose the story of the crossing into the Promised Land.

When the whole nation had finished crossing the Jordan,
the LORD said to Joshua, "Choose twelve men from among
the people, one from each tribe, and tell them to take up
twelve stones from the middle of the Jordan from right
where the priests stood and to carry them over with you
and put them down at the place where you stay tonight."

So Joshua called together the twelve men he had appointed from the Israelites, one from each tribe, and said to
them, "Go over before the ark of the LORD your God into
the middle of the Jordan. Each of you is to take up a stone
on his shoulder, according to the number of the tribes of
the Israelites, to serve as a sign among you. In the future,
when your children ask you, 'What do these stones mean?'
tell them that the flow of the Jordan was cut off before the
ark of the covenant of the LORD. When it crossed the
Jordan, the waters of the Jordan were cut off. These stones
are to be a memorial to the people of Israel forever."

So the Israelites did as Joshua commanded them. They
took twelve stones from the middle of the Jordan, according to the number of the tribes of the Israelites, as the
LORD had told Joshua; and they carried them over with
them to their camp, where they put them down. Joshua set
up the twelve stones that had been in the middle of the
Jordan at the spot where the priests who carried the Ark of
the Covenant had stood. And they are there to this day.

                                        Joshua 4:1-9 NIV

As we prepared to "cross over" from one point in our history
to another, we gathered our "rocks." We said, "This is what we
are going to take with us, and this is what we are going to leave
behind." We discussed the different types of things that we might
leave behind—attachments to things that were not necessarily of
God and attachments to whatever we thought might happen. We
emphasized our willingness to move with risk into an unknown
future with the understanding that we needed to take with us
those rocks of God's presence and the representations of God's
activity that would provide for us a framework for a healthy con-

gregation in the future. We took the baptismal font, the cross, the Bible, and the representation of the altar; we took the musical instruments and the ways in which we offered up praise. Children and youth led the procession, taking us out to our cars. As a community together, we talked about Moses leading people into the wilderness, into a time of unknown, and we went in a procession to our new facility. We gathered outside. As we stood, we talked about crossing the Jordan, how it was done not under the people's own power, but under God's power, reminding us that we weren't to revel in our accomplishments so much that we forget that it is actually God's accomplishment. This was our perspective as we walked in community together into the building.

A child cut the ribbon to remind us that we are not there simply for adults but for those generations who are yet to come. As we entered, we connected again with the scriptural story of God's glory.

> "Now, my God, may your eyes be open and your ears attentive to the prayers offered in this place.
> "Now arise, O LORD God, and come to your resting place,
> you and the ark of your might.
> May your priests, O LORD God, be clothed with salvation,
> may your saints rejoice in your goodness.
> O LORD God, do not reject your anointed one.
> Remember the great love promised to David your servant."
> When Solomon finished praying, fire came down from heaven and consumed the burnt offering and the sacrifices, and the glory of the LORD filled the temple.
> 2 Chronicles 6:40-7:1 NIV

There in that place on that day we had an opportunity to renew our baptismal vows, to discuss what it is to be forgiven by God's grace, to move into a time of servanthood, to be connected to the ancient story that gives us newness of life.

Every element of this process connected multiple forms of media, multiple dimensions of story, with the story of the Scripture woven into our current experience. We became not simply people who built a new building, but also people who continue in the line of those who went before. And like those who entered into the Promised Land, we were open to a future that God was creating even as we moved through that experience. This common memory and identity has become a part of the sacred story that shapes the congregation as they face future transitions.

In some ways, the visual leader is like the prophet Ezekiel, pointing to the future God desires and trying to rally the people to unify and move in that direction. Yet the visual leader isn't always specific and directive. Sometimes instead of painting the picture of the future we invite others into the living story of God. A helpful example of this shift is perceived in the final days of Moses' leadership. God had given Moses the vision of the Promised Land, but Moses didn't get to bring the people into that place. In his last act of leadership he pointed people toward a future into which he could not go.

> Then Moses climbed Mount Nebo from the plains of Moab to the top of Pisgah, across from Jericho. There the LORD showed him the whole land—from Gilead to Dan, all of Naphtali, the territory of Ephraim and Manasseh, all the land of Judah as far as the western sea, the Negev and the whole region from the Valley of Jericho, the City of Palms, as far as Zoar. Then the LORD said to him, "This is the land I promised on oath to Abraham, Isaac and Jacob when I said, 'I will give it to your descendants.' I have let you see it with your eyes, but you will not cross over into it."
>
> Deuteronomy 34:1-4 NIV

He went to the top of the mountain. He knew he was not going to be able to go into that Promised Land. He saw the future, but he didn't just see the future and say, "This is what's going to happen." He saw the future, came back down, and knew he wasn't to be the one who participated in all of it. What did he do? He reminded everyone of their connection to the palette of history and the power of God. He then painted a picture of where they were to move. Since they had that sense of connection with the past, that sense of continuity through story and history and the power of God, they were able to see the vision that he was painting of the future with much more purpose and much less anxiety. Joshua was able to pick up and lead where Moses was not able to go, because Moses had gone to the horizon. He had seen the future and painted a clear picture of their path. His act freed others to take up the vision and move forward.

The task of the leader is holding in careful tension the powerful pieces of the past, emerging visions that are being created, and the future that is yet to become. In that dynamic tension between past and future, there is a power and an energy that enable faithful, purposeful movement into the preferred future without jettisoning the richness of heritage.

To consider as you lead:

1. Think about your current leadership situation. What biblical stories, images, and metaphors come to mind?

2. How might you help those you lead see themselves as part of God's ongoing story? How could they paint themselves into the continued story of God's redeeming work in the world?

3. What are the things out of your history that support and point in the direction of the vision for the church?

4. What are the fears or anxieties that people are experiencing that might be keeping them from seeing the preferred future?

5. How might you help them connect to the past as a foothold to the future?

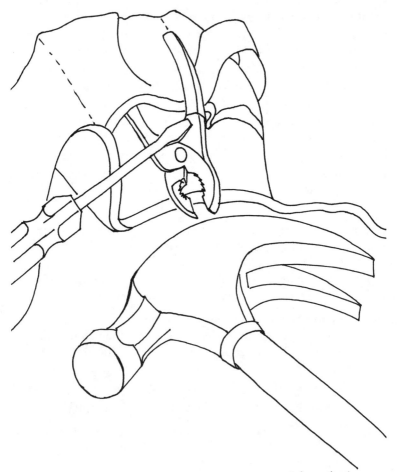

C. BennettBollinger

CHAPTER NINE

Changing of the Method, Changing of the Mind

During seminary, while on internship, I served as a general associate pastor in a medium-sized church in the Deep South. The pastor at this church provided me with a challenging experience and allowed me to become involved in and exposed to just about every area of the activities of ministry in the life of the congregation. While my supervisor was a very effective minister, there was a joke about him around the church (that I think he fed and kept alive) about his capacity to repair things. If anything broke around the church, or wasn't working properly, people would say, "Oh, tell the preacher to get his hammer; he can fix anything." It didn't matter what the problem was, from a leaky faucet to a malfunctioning piece of sensitive electronic equipment, the call was always for the man who could fix anything with the hammer. Of course no one would really let him near the equipment with the hammer, which is probably why he kept the joke alive; so someone else would be called on to fix the thing. After all, it was obvious that every particular situation was different and required different knowledge, different skills, and different tools.

Ezekiel goes multimedia

In Chapter One we briefly examined Ezekiel's use of symbolic action. Ezekiel 4:1-3 further develops this interesting, alternative method of communication. He engaged in a type of religious metaphorical street theater in order to cause the people to "hear" his message in a different way. No doubt the people in the streets had heard all the woe and judgments before. Other prophets proclaimed the anger of God and the destruction of the people. There were signs of the presence of the wrath of God in the form of invading armies and deportations, yet even in the midst of this apparent impending doom, even in a foreign land, the people did not really receive the message. They saw signs of the continuation of the life to which they were accustomed and so inferred that their lives would soon get back to normal and all would be well.

In the middle of this general denial about the extent of their exile, Ezekiel was given a method of communicating that relied on the power of *image*.

> "Now, son of man, take a clay tablet, put it in front of you and draw the city of Jerusalem on it. Then lay siege to it: Erect siege works against it, build a ramp up to it, set up camps against it and put battering rams around it. Then take an iron pan, place it as an iron wall between you and the city and turn your face toward it. It will be under siege, and you shall besiege it. This will be a sign to the house of Israel."
>
> Ezekiel 4:1-3 NIV

What are the elements of this symbolic action?

❖ **Using a clay tablet:** The clay tablet was a material commonly used in Babylon, both for building and for recording information. Ezekiel used a "form of media" from the context of the community into which the people had been exiled.

❖ **Drawing the city of Jerusalem:** The action of representing things by drawing was a practice common to the people of Babylon but not to the Hebrews. Ezekiel used a method from the context of the community into which the people had been exiled.

❖ **Building models of war equipment and arranging them around the drawing**: Ezekiel created an interactive physical representation of the event he was trying to portray in order to involve the people on a more experiential level.

❖ **Using an iron pan**: The prophet used an object that would be commonly understood as impenetrable by the audience.

❖ **Using the pan to separate the face from the model and drawing**: The prophet combined the image of impenetrability with the model of the event he was trying to portray, adding another dimension to his communication.

❖ **Without looking at the model (view blocked by the pan), enacting the siege of the drawing on the tablet**: He then participated in the action of the event, demonstrating at once the devastation of the city and the impenetrable wall that separated the face of God from the situation of Jerusalem.

This is a bizarre set of activities for a priest of the Temple of God to be carrying out on the street in front of the passers-by. Yet, the method of communication and the elements selected seem to have been chosen for their ability to communicate on a different level. What appears to be a simple action of illustration, recorded in three verses of Scripture, contains a complexity of layered imagery, method, and media to evoke in the hearer a richer understanding by engaging him or her on multiple levels simultaneously. Through this layered image-oriented communication, much more information was communicated in a relatively short period of time and communicated in such a way as to engage the hearers experientially.

This activity of creating meaning-laden, multidimensional spectacle is the proclamation method used by Ezekiel. He uses methods of communication that speak on a different level, and he uses materials (media) that were from the surrounding hostile culture. *ImageSmithing* is understood as the way in which

Ezekiel draws from a variety of sources and combines them into the creation of a multidimensional image, which provides a larger vision and an imaginary context for living, a context that frames the followers in the context of the larger story.

Image captures their attention. Image engages and creates their common memory. It provides for a shared sense of identity as the people of God, even though they are shattered and separated geographically and experientially. The creation of such an image also begins to build the heart of their reviving community, a vision of a common future and thus, a new motivation that springs from the hope that God is drawing them into a different kind of future. The future into which they are being drawn is not something that they are responsible for on their own, or something that they would venture into alone. It is a future that is already inhabited and prepared by God. The image created by Ezekiel is the voice of the grace of God calling to the people from the future Kingdom, which for them is still on the horizon, but which for God is already in existence.

The parallel between Ezekiel's task and ours is the need to use unorthodox multisensory forms of communication in order to get and keep the attention of those who are listening, to speak at once on a variety of levels so that diverse listeners get the message. As leaders of congregations we find ourselves in this kind of alien Diaspora. How are we to communicate and how are we to lead in the context of such diversity? We need to begin by understanding some of the changes that are taking place.

The new language, the new learner, and their challenge to the leader

We are experiencing tremendous changes all around us, and some of the biggest changes are in the ways we communicate.

I remember the old "Royal" black manual typewriter that sat on my father's desk in our house in Atlanta. It was big and heavy, and many thoughts were articulated at the intersection of key and fingertip. Words. Words printed in a form in which those words were tied together with a combination of knowledge, ability, skill, faith, wisdom, calling, and determination. The end result was a document, which served as the user-interface to the process of thought, study, reflection, experience, and analysis. I remember the little blue portable electric typewriter when it arrived. There was a time when it was questionable if its residence on the desk would be long term, because it was so much more "sensitive to the touch" and had a different "feel." But it stayed.

Another change came when the first computer made its way into the house. Wow! One of the things we noticed was that there were no longer any of those little correction tapes, wheel-brush type erasers, or carbon paper. The use of language and the medium of communication were the same—the conveying of meaning through words transmitted through fingertip—and the product was the same (the ink-on-wood-pulp-user-interface), but the process of manipulating the basic units of communication, the letters and words had taken on a new form. Separated from their physical presence on a page, the words were freed from the constraint of physical location. They became free to be shifted, changed, rearranged, and copied. The transformation of the method of manipulation of the basic unit of communication—letters and words—changed the transfer of knowledge a great deal.

The changes were not simply the absence of the prior tools of physical manipulation of the building blocks of language (erasers and correction tape). The nature of the thought process and communication itself changed. The act of writing, which previously required a much more reasoned, careful, and planned approach (once it was on the paper, you had to retype the whole thing to change it) became a creative and exploratory process. This is not to say that there was not creativity, or exploratory thought before, but the act of writing itself, touching fingertip to key, previously held much more of a sense of finality and commitment. As the building blocks of communication took up residence in the electronic realm, rather than in the physical, they allowed for more freedom of creative exploration, with less risk of the anchor, of the finality of physical commitment. The building blocks entered the electronic world. The blocks were the same, the interface between fingertip and key were the same, the final user interfaces were the same, but there had been a subtle shift in the mental approach to process of thought and written communication.

The world of word and letter accessed through the user interface of ink-on-wood-pulp will be around for a long time (25 years?), and should be, for it is an effective means of communication. Methods for engaging in the act of the manipulation of letters and words will continue to evolve. There are continued developments of speech-to-text technologies and screen-based personal electronic devices like the palm computer. I can imagine that they will soon emerge from the convergence of technologies, providing not only wireless access to the Internet, telecommunications, mp3 music files, and the ability to capture and distribute still and video images, but also access to online libraries filed with electronic books and articles and "papers." The world of the textual expression of human thought will become searchable and researchable, with immediate access and without the constraints of physical location.

The world of textual communication will continue to exist while undergoing radical transformation in the methods of manipulation of the building blocks and the nature of the interface. Shifts continue to take place all around us in the nature of the building blocks used for the transmission of information and meaning, as well as in the way the mind is developing in its process of comprehension. There are shifts in the world of communication that are far more radical, with extreme implications for the leader in the church today. These shifts have to do with the communication of meaning through the building blocks of *image*.

I remember in college a conversation with another student, and wanting to communicate a particular experience: a convergence of thought and the existential presence of being in the thought (which is very different from the thought itself, separate from the experience). I remember saying, "I wish I had a 'brain recorder' so I could just record my experience and share it with you." As I look back on it, I think that those words were the cry of a mind that was becoming oriented toward communication through images rather than through linear text. This orientation is born out of the tendency of the brain to adapt its comprehension strategies to the changing universe, constantly seeking to engage its world in the best way it can, and the emergence and proliferation of TV, video games, computers, and the dramatic increase of the film industry's ability to create images beyond the scope of normal reality. Because of this shift, my brain is wired differently from the brains of my parents. Because of this shift and subsequent mental adaptations to new developments in the language of image creation and distribution, my son's brain will be wired or stimulated differently (in terms of preferred communication) from mine.

I can almost hear Jonathan saying, when he is older, "Can you remember when you used to have to have a cell phone, a pager, a laptop, a camera, a radio and a TV before they were all part of these little wireless 'things' we now wear to send and receive our information through the on-demand world-wide information network?"

It boggles the mind to consider the transformation in the brain's ability to access and comprehend vast amounts of data and information that will be present as my son matures. As we stand in the midst of the emergence of a new way of knowledge and communication, I recall the words of Louis Armstrong, "*[He'll] learn much more than I'll ever know, and I think to myself, 'What a wonderful world.'* "

Consider Ezekiel's situation and his form of communication with the people of Israel there in the streets of the province of Babylon. He had a changed, changing, diverse, and scattered group with whom he was called to communicate. His situation called for a new method of communication. In response to the task, God had Ezekiel pull out all the stops. He used every type of communication in his portfolio and a couple that weren't. In the next chapter, we shall review some tools and techniques that are available to the ImageSmith today.

C. Bennett Bollinger

CHAPTER TEN

Leading by Layering with Multiple Tools and Techniques

In first grade I had a box of eight, horse-leg-sized crayons, primary colors and a few more, and I was able to use those crayons to draw simple pictures. There was a limited color palette with which I painted. As time moved forward, however, I recall the amazing moment when I received my first box of sixty-four crayons and a new horizon was opened up for creative potential. Not only was there green, but there were so many hues of green. A tree could be represented in spring green as well as in its middle-of-the-summer deep green. Water could be displayed not only as blue, but also as aquamarine, indigo, and many more hues. For a while, because I was familiar with the same old colors, I almost wore those crayons out, until I begin to step out and realize that much more could be created if I used all sixty-four crayons. The same richness of color is available as we begin to look at leadership possibilities and responsibilities for our congregations in the twenty-first century. Our box of crayons, our media forms, have increased dramatically in the range of colors.

Digital visual

Advertisers, as evident in one TV commercial, are crafting their message to reach a new "generation" of people. The generation is not defined by age or geography, but rather by the shared adaptation to the emerging realm of experience, communication, entertainment, and commerce. They are called "Generation D," or the digital generation. The commercial shows pictures of people young and old using various forms of digital media: music, pictures, video and communication. Ready or not, some of us are the digital generation.

I carry a backpack just about everywhere I go. When I was in seminary, I had books, paper, and a micro-cassette recorder. My primary means of communication were the written and the spoken word. Now, I carry two things in the backpack that are a big part of my ministry in this changing time. I carry my laptop computer and my digital video and still camera. For Ezekiel, the power of the image transcended the scattered diversity of his "congregation." The power of the image is crucial for us as well. In the laptop, I have several books including the Bible and study materials as well as word processing, image and video editing, and projection software.

As I think about teaching, preaching, vision casting, and leading the congregation, I am learning to live my life with an eye for images that communicate. Having the digital video/still camera with me gives me the ability to capture images and store them wherever I am. Frequently I will come across something that catches my eye, so I shoot it and save it. Later, I can share the images with the congregation, so they too can experience them through the media of new technology. The new digital media is one of my tools. We must have a variety of instruments in our tool kit for painting. We must be able to see those images and be ready to experience and share those images. As leaders use media forms to frame windows that peer into an ordinary experience of God, members of the congregation gain an extraordinary imagination that helps them practice spiritual disciplines and envision God's future expecations.

While in California our family visited Legoland. Legoland is a theme park where all the rides appear to be made with giant Lego blocks. While we were there, I was watching my boy ride the safari jeep ride. He was in the jeep having a great time, pretending he was on the safari and fully enjoying the experience. Directly behind him was a woman who appeared to be forty to forty-five, in the jeep, not holding onto the steering wheel, just sitting on the moving jeep as if it were a bench. As the jeep was rolling along, she was carrying on a conversation on her cell phone, her face expressionless. The contrasting image seemed so interesting to me that I took pictures of her and of my son. Not long after that trip, I was speaking on *"Unless you become like little children, you will never enter the Kingdom of Heaven."* That pair of pictures communicated more deeply than an hour of written and verbal explanation about the way in which adults become distracted and miss being joyfully present to the good gifts of God.

How one church reduced resistance to placing a projector in the sanctuary

Most people are living in a digital world of images and are receiving much of their information and entertainment through the media. Many do a large portion of their shopping online, but it seems that in many settings, people are resistant to bringing digital media into the church. The screen is associated with TV and therefore somehow seems profane and not something that should be in the church. This is a predictable resistance to change and things that are new.

When I was working with one particular church, helping them plan and develop the use of some newer forms of technology in the worship area, the pastor told me that he expected to have significant resistance from some of the older members of the church. Because he felt like it was the right thing to do, he was ready to move forward and take the heat. I suggested a different approach. I suggested that he reframe the situation to help church members make friends with technology instead of having a fight over it.

People don't mind technology if they can see its human side. Mother's Day was coming up, and at this particular church it has been a tradition for the children to color pictures and write prayers for their mothers and grandmothers. The pastor had the children make the cards the week before. He took pictures of the children with the digital camera as they were making the cards. Later he scanned into the computer all of the cards they had

made. He combined the pictures and images of the cards and projected them as the children sang. Immediately, the technology was
seen as something that helped them experience humanity and
love. Instead of being feared, on Mother's Day it was embraced.

Layered storydwelling and storytelling

For centuries, leaders have used a single media form for communication, either the written form or the spoken word to share
important ideas. Music and other arts have been used to add to
the dimensions of a particular experience in worship. However,
currently the situation requires a multimedia format. People are
used to receiving images on the television screen along with the
written word, video, and other graphic imagery. Spoken words,
music, image, color, light, and sound all combine to evoke experiences that are both intellectual and emotional.

The multisensory budget revival

I am frequently asked, "What do you do if you don't have a pro-
jector or a camera, and can't afford a computer with
PowerPoint®?" The response is that you use what you have.
Multisensory communication and ImageSmithing are not tied to
a particular piece of equipment. The possibilities for using digital imagery to enhance communication and experience are virtu-
ally endless, but this shift into experience is not just new media;
the ImageSmith draws with all sixty-four crayons. The key
requirements are creativity and resourcefulness.

When I was appointed to my first congregation, I felt out of
place. I had lived in Atlanta, Jackson, Denver, Heidelberg,
Germany and Oxford, England. I was appointed to a town that
had fewer than 2,000 residents. The church was almost 140 years
old. The people were wonderful, but I think they were a little
unsure of me as well. One of the members was having a conversation with his niece (who is now the business administrator of

the church I am serving). The niece asked, "So how's the new preacher?" His only response was, "He wears sandals..." I faced a steep learning curve in that first congregation.

One of the things I had to learn was how to do a revival. Having grown up in a large church with a formal liturgy on a university campus, I hadn't been exposed to a revival. I was rather sure that we needed music and preaching, and that it was supposed to be something that would, well, revive you, or the church, or something. I called my intern supervisor (the one who could fix everything with a hammer) to preach. He had done revivals before, so he was my ace in the hole. Then I set to work on designing the service.

At the time I didn't know anything about multisensory worship or communication. I had been trained (much like Ezekiel) to maintain things in the Temple. But, I did have a background in theater. How about the dry bones scripture from Ezekiel as a theme for the revival? After all, those bones certainly were revived. And how can we help people who have heard this scripture a thousand times experience it in a fresh way so that it can have the desired effect? And an idea started to come to me. (You should be reminded that I am recently graduated from seminary, the fall directly following my arrival.)

The opening night of the revival was upon us. People began filling the church. They knew what to do even if I was winging it. I stood up, in my robe, and welcomed everyone to the first night of the revival. Then I walked down the steps and left the sanctuary. I caught a couple of strange looks on the way out.

As soon as I was out of the room, I had someone shut off all the lights. It was instantly pitch dark. So that people wouldn't begin to panic or think something was horribly wrong, I immediately began to read the passage of Scripture (Ezekiel and the dry bones) through a wireless microphone from my office. Someone was stationed up in the balcony waiting the cue. It was one of those old wooden balconies with a flat floor and gray pull dividers so we could use the space for Sunday school rooms. We had taken a big plastic five-gallon pickle bucket, and filled it with a totally disassembled croquet set—wooden balls, mallet heads and mallet handles. It was in the balcony. When I got to the part about the dry bones beginning to rattle, the bucket man in the balcony began to rattle the croquet pieces in the bucket. From above and behind, as they sat in the darkness, they heard a rattling. As I reached the part where the bones came together, bone upon bone and joint upon joint, the bucket bearer, who had continued to rattle, now began to pour all of the pieces slowly out onto the wooden floor while gradually raising the bucket higher and higher so that the sound of the croquet pieces hitting and rolling across the second story wooden floor would increase in volume.

When Ezekiel began to prophesy to the bones and God was breathing into them, we started the tape of the song that one of the youth was going to sing. The intro was a blowing wind and a slowly building orchestral crescendo. As the Scripture text finished, and the crescendo on the tape's introduction reached its climax, all the lights burst back on and the youth, with a beautiful and powerful voice, jumped into "Sing Your Praise to the Lord." I walked back into the worship area as the young woman was singing. I looked at the congregation. Their eyes were wide open and their hair was standing up...or so it seemed...but they had heard the Scripture text in a new way and that Scripture set the background and established the context for a good series of services.

We didn't have projectors or expensive hardware, but with an inexpensive wireless microphone, a five-gallon bucket and a croquet set, balls, mallet ends and handles all disassembled, we had revival. In this case we used the same kind of imagination as a radio drama team. Creativity, resourcefulness, and the intent to communicate or reinforce the message on multiple levels are the only requirements.

Let us bake bread together...

One example of a multisensory experience took place over two days. We have developed a children's worship team to allow children to participate in the creation of the worship service. If they have opportunities to help create and lead, they feel much more a part of the experience. Another goal for the team is that children learn to think and look at the world calling forth images of God's story. On this occasion, we were helping the children experience and understand the sacrament of communion.

The children met one evening at the church in the kitchen. One of our members who is a chef had prepared all the ingredients for baking bread. When the children arrived, the chef had them wash up and then everyone got to participate in mixing up the dough. When the dough was ready, they all got to knead it. (They really got into the kneading part.) While they were cooking I took video and digital pictures of them; close-ups of flour-covered hands, smiling faces, and whole bodies. While the bread was baking, we sat at the table, and I told several of the bread stories in the Bible. We shared the story of the unleavened bread in Exodus. We talked about the way God provided manna in the wilderness. We talked about Jesus and the Last Supper. While we were sharing the stories, we could smell the bread baking.

When we finished the stories, we gathered in the sanctuary, and we talked about what a sacrament is and how it is something we do that connects us to all these stories and to the sacrifice of Christ. Before long, one of the helpers in the kitchen brought us some bread and a chalice. I asked the children if they wanted to help serve communion that weekend. We talked about how serious it was and that they needed to be focused on what they were doing. After letting everyone hold the bread and the cup and look into the eyes of the one being served, we shared communion, prayed, and everyone headed home.

That weekend at the service, I described what the children had done, the bread that we baked, and the stories we shared. As the parents listened, they heard the stories too. While I was talking, on the screen behind me were images of floured hands and dough and smiling faces. When it came time to share the sacrament, and the children came forward to serve, taking the bread they had baked from the table, they were ready. They took their places, looked deeply into the eyes of the person being served and told them the story… "This is the body of Christ, broken for you." "This is the blood of Christ, shed for you…" All of the elements that weekend came together, and the Word became flesh, incarnate within us. I don't think that those children will ever look at communion the same way again... nor will the rest of the congregation. The community came together into a deeper awareness, and developed a common memory based in a new experience of a traditional practice. This type of convergence is the work of an ImageSmith.

Living leadership lessons

While teaching about transformation is important, there is nothing more powerful than the witness of a transformed life. Part of the task of the ImageSmith is to catch people living out expressions of the transformed life and lift up their story as an example. Some churches interview people during the service and allow the congregation to "overhear." Some tell the stories of people. Video interviews and testimonies have played an important part in our congregational experience. Allowing people to share what God is doing in and through their lives, stories of personal awakening, transformation, and growth help provide an image of the reality of God at work. As people see these images they are able to look at their own lives with eyes towards transformation. And through the living lesson, they often can find encouragement and direction.

The idea is to catch someone living out a changed life, not only to compliment them but to hold that example up before people—not to say that you should do this or this is the way you have to behave, but to help people see the positive possibilities of living in that particular way. They can see not only the positive possibilities of living in that particular way for their own lives but also the positive possibilities of living in that way for the community of faith and the people of God and the future that could come into being. Because they see people behaving in a way that is preferred, they catch a glimpse of what it could be for their own lives. This is an important way to provide leadership.

The possibilities for using different media forms for communication and education are practically limitless. The only requirements again are creativity and a willingness to experiment. It helps to have people who are familiar with new media to help in the process. While you may think that you don't have anyone who knows how to use computers or digital cameras, or video editing software, the truth is that these skills are becoming more common, especially among the youth. When adults ask youth for help, it helps the youth to get involved in the process and to get excited about what they are doing. You may want to consider gathering some youth together and asking them to brainstorm ideas about different creative ways to communicate a Bible lesson or a sermon. But be ready and flexible; if you ask them to be creative, they will!

C. Bennett Bollinger

CHAPTER ELEVEN

Storydwellers and Storytellers

When I was in Atlanta for the 1996 Olympics, I witnessed an important event. I was standing on the curb at the corner of North Decatur Road and Clifton, near Emory University, with my parents, my wife, and my son, waiting for the torch to pass. There in front of us stood the runner who would receive the relay and continue the race. The torchbearer-to-be seemed somewhat nonchalant about the situation, chatting with other people around him. We stood and waited for a long time. Something had happened, and the prior runner had been delayed. As the waiting continued, people became distracted. Some even got discouraged and went home. Finally, we heard sounds from the distance, and then we saw the beginnings of the group that was traveling with the torchbearer. The air of excitement returned. As the runner approached there rose great cheering in the crowd. The torch that was making its way around the world was no longer just some isolated story that was being watched through the lens of the TV screen. It was here. It was now. It was real.

The change in the emotion of the crowd was tangible. People became focused and eyes brightened. We became clear about what was happening. The flame came closer and closer. I watched the eyes of the one who was preparing to receive the handoff of the torch. The expression that had been nonchalant became one of wide-eyed anticipation. The torchbearer drew nearer. It seemed as if everything went to slow motion. I watched the runner poised for the handoff. Suddenly, in his eyes, the moment became real. The torch that had been carried around the world, the torch that had been carried down through the ages, the torch that was being watched by millions of people from all over the world was about to be passed into his hand. He started to run, looking back over his shoulder, ready to take the hand-off without missing a step. The other runner came near. The torch was passed into the new runner's hand. His eyes were filled with concentration and seriousness. He knew that all eyes were on him. He didn't want to drop it. He didn't want to choke. He took hold of the torch, and his head began to turn down towards the road that stretched out before him. He looked forward at the next phase of the torch's journey, knowing that it was his turn to carry. The serious expression on his face gave way to a glowing brightness, and a beaming appearance of joy and responsibility. With eyes bright, a huge smile, head and torch held high, the torch-bearer ran down the road. We watched until he was out of sight.

I think of the torchbearer and the passing of the flame when I consider our situation and our task as people of God. The story of God's creative and redeeming activity, which has passed around the world and down across the centuries, now finds its way to the street corner of space and time where we live. We've heard the stories and they have had an effect on others across the years, but suddenly they are drawing near. Suddenly, in all of their flaming immediacy, the stories are handed to us and it is our turn to carry them forward.

In part, the visual leader is to help people see themselves as bearers of the story. If we as leaders are to be effective in helping people grasp the reality of who they are in God and how they are to be active parts of living God's future into being, it is important that we have an understanding of the role and task of all Christians, and a willingness to pass on the *work*, the *responsibility*, and the *joy*. The ImageSmith paints, then, and invites others to join the creative process.

Create a community of storydwellers and storytellers

We tell stories, and then the stories begin to "tell" us. My son Jonathan and I love to tell stories. We tell them when we are playing, and we tell them when we are going to bed. We make up a setting, create characters and a plot, and then insert our own characters into the story. Then comes the adventure. We make it up as we go along. One of us tells part of the story and the other one continues it. Once we were involved in telling stories of creatures that live in the digital world. We would lie in bed at night and build the story, adventure after adventure. We made the characters and then told the adventure a little more each night. We would always end the evening with the words "to be continued..."

During one particular part of an adventure as we lay in bed one evening, we came upon a cave painting that we had seen behind a waterfall in a cave. It was an image of several creatures standing on the top of a hill holding up their swords and staffs. We didn't know it as we told the story, but when we got to the final climax of the story and we had overcome the enemies, we (in the story) were standing on top of a hill holding up swords and staffs. As we stood there, *we narrated,* "and they remembered the image they had seen in the cave painting so long ago. The victory is ours..." That image became the image for the story. It told of the coming triumph that would be ours, even when the going seemed tough. That was not really the intended outcome of the story. It merely happened extemporaneously as we told it.

During the following January, I was coming out of a particularly hectic Christmas season. We had experienced some tragedy in the church, and some other very difficult things had happened. I was scheduled to spend a week in school in California, and I would get off schedule with work on my degree if I postponed this week. I decided to go on to school and get on with the process. While I was out there I received some news of more difficult things that some people were going through back at the church, and I heard of the possible divorce of one of my close friends. The news hit me hard, and I considered throwing up my hands, giving up on the degree, and getting the next plane back home. I went back to my room and started throwing things into my suitcase, in case I decided to go. As I was arranging things in my suitcase, I found, folded into my clothes, a piece of light green paper with the artwork of my seven-year old. He had drawn a picture of those characters from our story—on top of the hill holding up their swords. Under the picture were the words "the victory is ours." Jonathan had no idea that I would be going through the difficulties I was encountering. He had no way of knowing that this picture would speak the words I needed to hear, at the right moment, but because he had lived that story, because he had been a story dweller, he became a storyteller, and that story took on a life of its own; it began to shape us beyond our own telling.

God's story is not merely something that we are to know about; it is something we live in, and stories receive their life as they are told over and over again. Also, people receive their life from stories as they become able to participate in the telling. As they join in the telling of the stories, the stories begin to shape them and the community.

Releasing the storytellers: telling "fish stories"

Jesus said, "Leave your nets, and from now on, you will fish for people." I saw a shirt once that continued this line of thought by going deeper into the fishing metaphor. The shirt said, "Simon Peter's tackle shop—you catch 'em, He'll clean 'em" (referring, of course to the act of evangelism and the subsequent newness of life through the justifying grace of God through Christ). Louisiana is a fishing state. We have bayous, lakes, streams, rivers, saltwater lakes, tidal rivers, and the Gulf of Mexico. Fishing is a huge industry here. While many people make their living by catching fish and shrimp, many also fish recreationally. In some areas you are not allowed to keep what you catch. These are called "catch and release" areas. While I understand Jesus' metaphor of fishing as evangelism, I understand the analogy in terms of "catch and release." The idea is not merely to draw people into a relationship with Christ (although that is a major part of it); our goal is to help people come to know their place in the story of God's unfolding grace and then release them to share that story with others in whatever way God has instilled their gifts.

Tell me the old story...

Stephen Ministry (www.christcare.com) is an important program in the life of our church. We provide people with fifty hours of training so that they will be able to listen to and provide care for people who are going through difficult times. One of the things that I have started doing with the Stephen Ministers in training is to sit with them and tell them a narrative overview of the story of God's activity in the world. I don't hit details, but rather I paint the flow of the story in broad strokes (creation, fall, calling a particular people, freedom from captivity, wandering, disobedience, law, Promised Land, division, exile, return, struggle, prophecy, the coming of the Messiah, life, death, resurrection, the beginning of the church, the spread and the corrections, continued struggle, and the promise of a future hope). Most of the time, those coming to participate in this ministry are familiar with the stories of the Bible, but most of them know Bible stories in relative isolation, rather than as a continuous narrative.

My goal during this exercise is to provide an overview of the Bible story that can provide a context for their helping work. I begin by telling the story, then I ask them to divide into pairs, and have them tell each other the story. At first, the reaction is usually one of approaching an impossible task: "I can't do that." "You have been to seminary." "There is no way we can remember all those stories." I encourage them to continue. If one person gets stuck, and forgets what comes next in the story, the other person can give him a hint. As they stop protesting and begin to tell one another the story, the attitude of the room changes. They concentrate. There are pauses, then thinking and searching. Inevitably, someone will grab a Bible and start to look something up. When they find what they are looking for, their eyes light up, "Oh yeah!" and they continue the storytelling. If people get really stuck, I help them out. It isn't a test; it is an exercise. If they can establish in their minds the framework of the Bible story as a whole, then they can set our lives and the lives of those they serve in the context of the unfolding story. By the end, they are all excited; each told the story to one another. If they have done it once, they will be able to do it again.

We want to catch people, as Jesus calls us to do, but not for the purpose of full nets or boats. We release people so that they can become tellers of fish stories as well. As more and more people understand that our world is the world of God's unfolding story, and as more and more people begin to tell and retell that story in the nuances that God has granted to each person's life, then the church—the people of God—will expand and grow.

Sometimes the story is shared verbally, sometimes through action, sometimes through image, and sometimes through art. Here are two living examples of the power of "catch and release" practices among storytellers and storydwellers.

The bent pansy and the new wine

One spring as the flowers started to bloom in Louisiana, we had been in our church building for a little over a month. We had used all of our money to build the building, and we had very little for furnishings. We decided that we needed the space and we could do with makeshift furnishings as we grew. We were using an office table that had been donated by a local hospital as an altar table, and we didn't have much money for altar decorations. On the way to church that morning, I had seen many beautiful flowers growing and blooming all over the place, and it occurred to me that people would appreciate the opportunity to use the flowers from God's creation to place on the altar. This would be an opportunity to participate in the life of worship. I announced during the worship service that if anyone wanted to pick flowers out of their yard or on the side of the road, they could bring them in and place them on the altar, which could be for us a symbol of God's gift and our recognition of God's handiwork. The next Sunday, as worship began, I had finished the words of welcome and announcements, and we had started to sing. One family came in a bit late with a little girl. She was holding in her hand a styrofoam cup with a pansy that she had picked (a pansy that looked well-loved by a little child). That pansy in a cup of water was brought to the front of the church during the singing as everyone was watching. She handed it to me, and without thinking about it much, I took it and I placed it on the altar, at the base of the cross.

Unknown to me was a woman visiting for the first time, a woman who was a florist and who had designed fantastic, immaculate, intricate flower arrangements for most of the large churches in the city and who had been involved in preparing flowers for weddings and funerals and all kinds of social events. Her perception of that particular moment rekindled a new future for her and an opportunity for the unfolding of God's gifts in many, many people. She saw a child placing her simple gift of a pansy into the hands of the worship leader, the leader recognizing that gift, and then placing it in a position of prominence. Because of that simple act, that woman experienced a strong openness to God and a desire to be part of a community that could see the simple gifts as that important. She decided at that moment this community is where she would like to share her gifts. She volunteered help with developing our worship centers and altar decoration.

Mary never merely decorates the altar/table area for the sake of adornment but always tries to allow the arrangement to be an extension of the theme of the worship service and the Scripture for the day. Her creativity adds a new dimension to the congregational experience of worship. And the creativity of expression and the telling of the story don't stop there. She now teaches people how to utilize their gifts in the creation of the altar. After a couple of years, she realized that her passion is teaching people creative expression through artistic altar design. She sold her floral business and started a school to help people use the gifts that God has given them in creating altars and images for use in worship by utilizing things that exist in nature. The school is called *New Wine Design.*[1]

A large and growing group of people participates regularly in the creation of our worship altars. Members of our altar design group have gone with Mary to create the altar and worship settings for some denominational meetings, and she has led workshops in several churches and denominational events. A little girl with a bent pansy wanted to share the gift of God's creative beauty in church, and her offer sparked the release of a large new wave of creativity in telling the story.

From the ashes

The first time Butch attended the church, I was preaching about our call to look beyond the walls of the church and to serve those who are suffering as we would serve Christ. I informed the congregation about a work-day in a nearby community to help people who couldn't help themselves, to fix up their houses. I told the congregation that our real worship and involvement takes place when our faith touches the world. Butch spoke to me later and said, "I have been to many churches, and they were always asking me to come and join. This is the first time I've come to church and had the pastor tell us all to leave: I knew that this was the church for me!" Butch became active in several of the mission and outreach projects of the church and was the lead carpenter when the congregation built a house for a woman who had been living in the ruins of a house with only a fifty-five-gallon drum and burning garbage for heat. He loves to work with wood, and he loves to serve God by serving others.

One day he came to my office with a gift. He had taken a piece of the top of an old wooden work table and carved the surface so that the letters and images stood out. The words read, "I slept and dreamed that life was joy. I woke and found that life was service. I served and found service, joy." He had taken a worn out piece of wood and through his art and even the medium for that art, had clearly expressed his theology. The broken and the worn can be restored into things of beauty and life, and that fullness of life is found in the activity of servanthood.

I found something else that would help release Butch as storyteller. While we were in England filming for *ReConnecting*, we went to St. Andrew's Parish Church in Epworth, where John

Wesley grew up. The first part of that church was built in the 1100s, the next part the 1200s, and finally the new part, the bell tower, was built in the 1500s. Approximately 200 years after the tower was constructed, a little boy was born to the priest of St. Andrew and his family. The little boy was John Wesley. John grew up in the area, heard the story of God, heard the story of the resurrection, heard the story of outreach to the world, and so gave his life to God in a way that ultimately a new movement in the Church was born. Today that movement is a denomination and several offshoots that reach around the world.

The bell tower had been struck by lightning a few years prior to our visit, and while we were there it was undergoing some much-needed renovations. Some of the wood from the damaged beams in the tower had been thrown on the ground and were lying in a pile near the dumpster. It had been 500 years since this wood had been taken from the tree. It was lying on the ground, crawling with bugs, and scarred by burned places. It looked to me like they were just going to get rid of it. So, I asked the rector if they were going to throw it away "Yes," he replied, "It is burned, old, and rotting." What he said was true but it looked a little different to me. I didn't just see burned and rotting wood. I saw the structure of story. "Could I have some?" I asked. The rector agreed, so we selected a couple of pieces.

We had a little rental car called a Mondeo. It was a very small European model Ford (about the size of an Escort wagon) filled with four people's luggage (two weeks' worth), and video equipment. We opened the back and rearranged things so we could cram in two of these giant beams. After several attempts, we finally got the back hatch closed, and we drove off to London with the rear end of the car dragging. I remember the look on the attendant's face when we walked into the "pack and ship," set the wood down on the counter and said, "We want to ship this wood to the United States. We want to insure it too." The poor guy looked at us in such a way that we heard him thinking, This is crazy. . .this is wood. You have forests in America. You can get wood in a forest without having to ship it airmail. Where are the hidden cameras? After a while he agreed to ship it.

We returned to the states, and the wood arrived at the church. I made a phone call. "Butch, I've got this 500 year-old wood here that came out of the bell tower in the church where John Wesley grew up, and I wondered if you might want to let God touch this wood through you and bring something out that would be a glory to God for 500 more years?" There was a long pause. He was both intrigued and fearful. He was intrigued because of the richness and the depth of the resource, and he was fearful because it was his turn to tell the story. It was his turn to carry the torch. All eyes would be on him, and he didn't want to choke.

If you were to ask Butch about his life, he would tell you that he had lived a rough life and experienced a lot of things where he got burned, broken, and cast aside. He wondered why he got the honor of this task. "Why do I get to participate in this unfolding 500-year history to bring praise and glory to God for another how ever many years?" Why? Well, I'll tell you why, because God takes the burned and the broken things and restores them. God *catches* us up in the story of creation and redemption and *releases* us to share that story with others in any way we can.

He took the wood and put it in his shop. He told me that he spent hours just looking at it. A couple of times, he asked me, "What do you want me to do with the wood? What do you want me to make?"

I answered, "Look at the wood, and listen to God, and see what God is calling forth from your heart and the heart of the wood."

Butch became more attentive in church. He appeared to listen more closely and with a sense of urgency. One day he came by the office and talked to me about prayer. He said, "You have been talking about the way that we are to pray and to draw close to God. Well, every time I try to pray and talk to God, I either ramble on, get selfish, run out of things to say, or my mind wanders."

I asked him, "Butch, when you are working with wood for a service project, do you feel close to God?"

"Oh yes," he replied, "closer than ever."

"Well," I said, "That is prayer. That is drawing near to God and participating with God in creation and the telling of the story of creation and redemption both in and through you."

His eyes lit up. He smiled. He looked at me with a sparkle and said, "You mean... that's prayer?!?"

"Yes. Prayer takes on many forms, but most importantly, it is communication and communion with God, and you find that in your wood work." He looked like a little boy who was getting away with something and being given permission to continue.

Butch studied the wood for months, and then, without a single electric tool, began to carve and shape the ancient wood. The knots in the wood became lion faces. Beneath them stands Daniel, with his gaze fixed upward beyond the danger. Vines intertwine as they climb up toward the top of the cross. At the center of the cross stands Jesus, not being crucified, but with his hands outstretched as if to say, "Come to me all you who are weary and heavy laden and I will give you rest," or he could be saying "Go into all the world and make disciples, baptizing them in the name of the Father, the Son, and the Holy Spirit, teaching them to obey all the things all I have commanded you" Above his head soars a dove, the presence of the Holy Spirit and the promise of peace, and behind all of it, lightly hammered into the wood are hundreds of interlocking circles that look to me like the great cloud of witnesses... the saints of the story of God. A burned and broken piece of wood lying on the ground waiting to be thrown away, waiting to be cast off, waiting to be burned or rot in a dump somewhere, became an act of prayer. And that which sat in a darkened tower and then on the ground now gets to stand and tell over and over the story of the resurrection of Jesus Christ.

Today, Butch works on building projects, teaching others how to build. He made a cross out of the same wood for a new church development in South Louisiana. He found the point of intersection between his life and the story, and as he understands it, he lives it, painting the story in the shavings of wood, and passing it on to generations yet to come.

As he participated in that transformative, creative activity, God was touching him and working a transformative, creative activity in his life. You see, Butch's story says, "I was burnt, I was broken, I was close to being thrown away. But God didn't give up on me. God gave me the opportunity to take a piece of wood with a 500-year heritage and bring forth something that is to the glory of God. God doesn't take broken stuff and throw it out. God redeems it and sets it free to tell others the story."

This storydwelling process isn't something that happens only with an old wood relic and a talented woodworker. As a visual leader, as an ImageSmith, I see it happening every day in and through the lives of videographers, artists, writers, florists, teachers, construction workers, musicians, medical personnel, lawyers, chemical dependency workers, and football coaches— the same kind of people who worship in your congregation. They each have in them the ability to tell the story of God's activity, and as they learn the story, see themselves in the story, and are released to tell the story to others, two things happen: 1) their faith grows, 2) and other people are drawn into the life of the ever-expanding story.

Rushing patiently

Sometimes patience is a difficult thing. Sometimes I see possibilities and I want to jump in and get with it, without taking the time to help others see what I see and get a handle on the purpose and direction of what we are about to do. This is one of the most important lessons I have learned. My job is not to make things happen or to draw people into what I want or what I think is best, but to help us as a community to see into God's story and to go where God is leading.

One of our church members owned some property out in the country. There was an old chapel on the land that was in disrepair, and she wanted to know if I thought the chapel was worth restoring and placing in our prayer garden. I thought it would be wonderful to take that dilapidated thing, bring it back to the Prayer Garden, fix it up, have the entire congregation focused on a common project. It could be a place of prayer. It would use the gifts, abilities, and resources of the congregation to take something old and transform it into something new. What a powerful example that would be. I saw it clearly.

Now here is where it became a problem. Before sharing the vision with others and helping people to see the possibilities and the benefits of the project, during a worship service I told the story of the chapel and what I wanted to do with it. Half the people in the congregation saw it immediately. They were in sync with what I was seeing, and were ready to move forward. The other half responded differently. They didn't see what I saw. They saw liability and expense. They saw a dilapidated chapel out in front of the new church building. I'm not sure what else they saw, but they told me that they weren't at all on board with that project.

This moment of conflict provided me with an opportunity for an important leadership decision. I could have gotten angry that these people didn't see what I saw so clearly, and set out to build support for my vision. I could have mustered enough supporters to force the vision through, but that would have caused division and pain within the congregation. Instead God was teaching me patience, and the need to allow the resources and the vision of the people to also help guide that process. I had to step back from that particular vision in the way and admit that I had seen it in a form that may never come into being. Yet as I let go of it— an important discipline, let go and trust God for God's timing— an amazing thing occurred.

One day I was visiting with someone who was contemplating going into ordained ministry. We were talking about what was the will of God, and we moved out into the Prayer Garden to have some time alone and to reflect. As we were walking, we were met by Wilton. (Wilton is a church member who works in the woods around the church every morning and has transformed a tangled underbrush into a place of prayer and meditation.) Now we were not looking to have a conversation with Wilton, but Wilton was there and we talked. I asked, "Wilton, how do you know the will of God?" He said, "Wow. That's a tough question. I'm not sure how you know the will of God, but the most important thing for me is to realize that it's not that I'm trying to get what I want done, or that I'm trying to get God to do what I want God to do, but instead that I am yielding so that my will recedes and the will of God becomes the directing force of my life."

Wow! I thought. Wilton spoke words that the one considering ordained ministry needed to hear. Wilton spoke words that I needed to hear as I stood there in that place. Then it was his turn to ask me a question. It had been almost a year since the chapel concept was broached, and I had set it down, let it go, but God had been dwelling in Wilton. He asked, "Where do you want the chapel?" He was not talking about the chapel that I had seen on the side of the road. He was talking about a chapel that he was beginning to cultivate out of the seed that had been planted earlier. I stood there with Wilton and the person considering ordained ministry, and we painted a picture together of a chapel that would stretch upward like the surrounding pine trees. Big windows would allow people to experience the natural beauty of the Prayer Garden, so that they would be able to see the creative processes of God in the seasons of nature all around them. As we shared the vision and articulated story, I felt a renewed sense of hope. That hope swelled even more when, on the following Sunday, I came out of church and started to drive away. I saw Wilton out there with a couple of other individuals from the church and a couple of children. He was painting into their minds the story of the chapel that was beginning to emerge through our shared vision and our shared experience of God.

Because I was able to let go, I didn't force something to happen that would have caused divisiveness or polarization in the midst of the congregation. Instead I released that idea, put trust in God, and a year later perceived how the story had taken root within God's creation.

Postscript: God is already there

Remember the story of the conch shell and the hermit crab from Chapter 1? I said that it seemed like a good story at the time, even though I wasn't sure if it was actually one of those inspired symbolic actions experienced by Ezekiel, or if it had merely been placed there by other circumstances, and I came across it fortuitously with a fertile imagination. Well, sometimes as a visual leader you put one story together with another, and the only sensible interpretation is to give God the credit for guiding your congregation.

In late 2001, I was upstairs in the youth room, leading a Discovering Grace session for a group of inquirers. Sione Tu'uta, our ministry intern from Tonga, was sitting in on the class. I was telling the story of the shell as I do every time to persons who are ready to learn why they might join our community in ministry. Afterwards, Sione walks up to me, and he's looking pale, "What's the matter?" I ask.

He reaches up to his powerful forearm, takes his sleeve and rolls it up. On his shoulder, there is a tattoo of a hermit crab and a shell. He then tells me that a traditional Tongan story for school children is the story of a life that develops, that must reach out beyond its own shell, into a risky environment, to become all that God can create this life to become. That symbol of the crab and the shell, he says, is the symbol for the Methodist Church in Tonga. And so when I tell the story of the shell to those who would become leaders in our community, I do not believe that it is merely an accident that I found a shell buried in pine straw on the land that we would inhabit. A skeptic might roll the eyes with a knowing sociological smile and assert that the visual leader, like founders and planters in other religious traditions, dreams these symbols or signs into explanatory stories. No, with full confidence I tell the future leaders that if God is active in the stories of our congregation, then don't you think that God is active in drawing you into your position of leadership at this time in your life? And, if God is already there and already active, then what we discover is a tremendous freedom and a sense of partnership with God as we seek to find our place in the story and tell it with all the resources that are available to us.

As I become more aware that we are living into a story that God is already inhabiting, I am developing an incredible sense of freedom to tell the story in new ways and release people to tell the story in ways that have yet to be imagined. I was at the Perkins School of Theology recently for a meeting of intern supervisors. We were discussing interesting developments in our congregations. I began to share what we were about to begin. I told them of a song we had shared in worship that had a wonderful percussion part, and the way in which many of our percussionists had played all at the same time. The song and the percussion section motivated Sione to tell us about Tongan drums. He described handmade drums of various sizes, and the groups of people who played them together. "I need to make some of those for the church," he said. "Where can I find a cow skin?" he asked. "The best bet is on a cow," I replied, being less than helpful. I really don't know much about where to get cowhide.

Later that afternoon, I was thinking about the drum dilemma, and it came to me that while we may not have many cattle herders in the congregation, we do have an abundance of deer hunters who accumulate deer skins throughout the season. That was it, I thought, we can combine the resources of the people here with the practices and talents of our associate pastor, and we will have something that tells the story in a creative and unique way. I went on to describe to the meeting of ministry intern supervisors the dream of teaching people in the congregation to build their own Tongan drums. "Think of it," I said, "Tongan deer drums for Jesus." The group laughed. I laughed too. Then I noticed that the director of the intern program had a serious expression on his face. I wondered if my levity had gone overboard.

After a moment, he spoke, "I don't know what is happening there, but if Tongan drums are being played at church in Shreveport, Louisiana, then there really is hope for the world."

Our churches are presently living in brackish water, dwelling between the pure and the salt water, in the rhythms of shifting tides. Visual leadership is the strategy that may best help your congregation to become a community of storydwellers and storytellers, who risk emerging from their shells, to navigate the waves and the currents ahead.

Remember to keep the light on

Imagine someone trying to paint without light. You give this person all the paints, all the paint brushes, everything, and put this person in a room where it is totally dark and say, "Paint this." It would probably not turn out like the painter had imagined it would. It would be very difficult to paint without being able to see. The horizon would be skewed. The foreground might replace the background. Perspective would be impossible because there is no perspective without light. The same is true in leadership. If you don't have the appropriate light, the source of power that comes beyond us, then you are likewise unable to paint the vision that God would convey. So how do you learn to leave the light burning? A spiritual connection must be wired into the life of the leader.

> Moses' face shone because he had been with God. When Moses came down from Mount Sinai with the two tablets of the Testimony in his hands, he was not aware that his face was radiant because he had spoken with the LORD.
>
> Exodus 34:29

This is the light that would be present in the images that you convey to God's people. If you are offering your dry spiritual leftovers, it will be difficult to motivate anyone to live into or retell the story. Remain open to God and spend time in the presence of God. As a leader divinely illuminated, you will be filled with the power to attract followers and to build community of storydwellers.

Notes

[1] See New Wine Design at www.newwinedesign.com.

Additional Resources from Grace Community Church

ReConnecting: A Wesleyan Guide for the Renewal of Our Congregation
By Rob Weber

ReConnecting is a seven-week or seven-session experience designed to get congregational small groups in touch with historical (Wesleyan) roots and contemporary cultural forces, so that an individual can embrace his or her "priesthood." Also an envelope for a church vision and for strategic planning used throughout a congregation and based in prayer and identity formation. The use of the seven-session experience may be customized based on the churches' vision and need—to simulate a frozen congregation, to deploy as an adult group Lenten activity, or to revisit a Wesleyan heritage.

Leader's Guide with DVD

Leader's Guide

Publication Date: 10/2002
ISBN: 0-687-02234-7
Price: $39.00

* Leader's Guide included on DVD as a PDF file (printed book contains text of the Participant's Guide)
* Promotional Video Trailer (a summary of the sessions).
* Customizable Poster (TIFF and PDF format)
* Publicity material (Sample letters, brochure, and registration card).

System Requirements:

DVD is compatible with all DVD set top players and many PC DVD-ROM players.

Participant's Guide
Does not include DVD.

Participant's Guide

Publication Date: 10/2002
ISBN: 0-687-06535-6
Price: $10.00

ReKindling: A Guide for Congregations with Multiple Or Alternative Worship Patterns
By Stacy Hood

Whether your church is looking to add to a traditional music program or start a nontraditional music ministry, *ReKindling Your Music Ministry* provides worship leaders advice on making an effective transition into a new music format by reducing or better managing conflict. The "key" ingredient in a music ministry is to focus hearts on doing God's will-which is an excellent antidote to anxieties about entertainment and performance in worship.

$10 eBook available from Cokesbury.com (Click "eBooks & eDocs" tab.)

For more information about [...], visit www.gracehappens.org.
For more information about Rob Weber, visit www.RobWeber.org.